Responsible Librarianship
Library Policies For Unreliable Systems

By David Bade

Responsible Librarianship
Library Policies For Unreliable Systems

By David Bade

Library Juice Press
Duluth, Minnesota

Copyright David Bade, 2006-2007

Library Juice Press
P.O. Box 3320
Duluth, MN 55803
http://libraryjuicepress.com/

Library Juice Press is an imprint of Litwin Books, LLC.

This book is printed on acid-free paper that meets all present ANSI standards for archival preservation.

Text design by Rory Litwin

Cover design by Topher McCulloch

Library of Congress Cataloging-in-Publication Data

Bade, David W.
 Responsible librarianship : library policies for unreliable systems / by David Bade.
   p. cm.
 Includes bibliographical references.
 ISBN 978-0-9778617-6-7 (acid-free paper)
 1. Machine-readable bibliographic data--Quality. 2. Online library catalogs--Quality. 3. Cataloging--Quality control. 4. Library catalog management. 5. Cataloging errors. 6. Bibliography--Methodology. 7. Online bibliographic searching--Evaluation. 8. Library cooperation. I. Title.
 Z699.35.Q35B33 2007
 025.3'132--dc22
                              2007046351

It did not entirely satisfy me to narrate wrongs;
I felt like denouncing them.
Frederick Douglass, *My Bondage, My Freedom*

Contents

Foreward! by Thomas Mann — ix.

A Note on This Edition — xiii.

Politics and Policies for Database Qualities — 1.

Letter to Autocat Concerning LC's Series Treatment Decision, May 31, 2006 — 109.

Structures, Standards and the People Who Make Them Meaningful — 115.

Appendix/Handout — 137.

About the Author — 173.

Foreward!

There is a kind of "code word" situation that has developed in the library profession in recent decades; it is manifested in an appeal to a set of beliefs that, while largely unarticulated, is nonetheless socially endorsed without a perceived need for argument or evidence. The evidence is assumed to be there; after all, when enough people share the same assumptions that support networks can be appealed to, those social networks functionally take the place of what, in other situations, would require considerable explicit justification. Were the "code words" actually based on the "science" part of "library science," then their adherents would have to realistically consider the possibility of falsifying evidence, of counter-examples, of whole bodies of literature to the contrary, and of the possible–perhaps radical–incoherence of their beliefs when situated in larger contexts of other beliefs known to be true via other tests. What matters with the "code word" mind set is not whether one examines possible falsifying considerations; what matters is simply whether one "gets it" or not. Fashion replaces argumentation.

Perhaps the most insidious of the "code" beliefs in the library profession today is the oft-repeated statement "We should not let *the perfect* stand in the way of *the good*"; or "The perfect is *the enemy* of the good." This assertion has various implications in practice. Most frequently it means that, particularly for library catalogers, "throughput time" or "speed" in turning out records is now to be considered "the gold standard" of quality. Despite a mountain of evidence to the contrary (*Cataloging and Classification Quarterly*, 23 [3/4], 1997), it is further assumed that "indexer consistency studies" demonstrate that trained catalogers don't agree with each other in any event, in the supposedly-perfect products they have been (vainly) trying to produce up to now. And therefore, it follows, consistency–i.e., standardization, categorization, authority work, cross-referencing, etc.–is not a realistic goal to pursue in the first place; instead, we just need more *transcribed* or *harvested* keywords taken from books themselves, that can be relevance-ranked (not standardized) by machine algorithms; or we just need more "tagged" keywords *added to* records by the general public, whose collective folk wisdom can replace (not supplement) subject experts who have actual knowledge, not just of the book (or other work) in hand, but of the larger context of its subject relationships to other works that are within, or related to, its own field. Neither relevance-ranking nor democratic tagging by non-librarians, of course, is expensive; neither requires *thinking* by library personnel. Neither requires any expensive professional work. Whether the needs of the library's users—particularly academic and scholarly users—are met by such processing procedures is irrelevant, because "the code" *also* assumes (without argumentation) that the very goal of cataloging is no longer to show "what the library has"—that is much too parochial a focus when there is an entire Internet out there with billions of things in it—but is, rather, to provide "something quickly"—and provide it especially to remote users outside library walls who are further assumed not to need any training or education in how to go about finding what they need. (The "under the hood" software manipulations of whatever keywords they type into "a single search box" will handle those problems for them.) Traditional library-access mechanisms will obviously not "scale up" to dealing with billions of records; so it follows that they must be simply abandoned (rather than having them continue to deal with a much more manageable subset of all informational records, such as the set of pesky *books* that keep being published each year.)

So: where do we go from here? I suspect many librarians will have visceral feelings that something is wrong with "the code" they hear so frequently repeated. Perhaps instead of endlessly repeating these assertions we should actually look at the evidence, either in their favor or falsifying them. That's where David Bade comes in. Bade, a cataloger at the University of Chicago's Regenstein Library, is a genuine scholar in the library profession. And he has done something that is rarely seen in library literature: he has read widely enough to examine library science as a whole in the context of related disciplines. He has immersed himself in the literature of high reliability organizations, human error studies, ergonomics, reliability engineering, and joint cognitive systems. He brings to bear a knowledge of philosophy, history—and even farming!—in his considerations of what actually *works* in libraries, and for *what purposes*. What he offers in this book is a coherent integration of what is, demonstrably, established knowledge from a wide variety of relevant fields, weighted not by machine algorithms but rather by a fine professional discrimination based on decades of actual experience in doing the work of librarianship. He combines the perspectives of a 30,000 foot overview with the necessary corrections that must be made, extensively and routinely, at ground level. A sure sign of a real scholar is his or her ability to provide concrete examples from that "ground level" experience, with an extended analysis of their further implications, not just out-of-context individual sentences cherry-picked from user surveys devised by people lacking that experience, who may have therefore failed to ask the right questions to begin with. Bade's extensive quotations from the literature he has researched–N.B.: extended quotations from, not just superficial footnote citations to–provide the rest of us with a coherent patterning and integration of knowledge that the library field so desperately needs at present. Bade offers not the "snippets" of information that quick and dirty searching offers, but a deep understanding that comes from his rare combination of very wide reading and very extensive personal experience, not just with the intentions, but with the results of the systems he's talking about.

"The perfect is the enemy of the good"? Perhaps, after reading this timely and much-needed study by David Bade, the library profession might actually consider a counter-proposition: "The even greater enemy of the good is the slipshod, the incompetent, the superficial, the incomplete, and the demonstrably incorrect."

Thomas Mann
Washington, D.C.

A note on this edition

The three papers reprinted here were written in the aftermath of the decision by the Library of Congress to cease providing authority records for series, a decision based upon the assumption that keyword searching in the LC catalog would provide sufficient access for series titles. The efforts previously expended on distinguishing and collating series through the establishment of authorized headings in authority records and the pairing of these with the forms actually found on the item being catalogued was deemed no longer necessary. It seemed to me at the time (as it does now) that such a decision is the prerogative of any institution, including LC, but that in the complex and integrated network of social and technical systems of libraries today, any decision to not do what all others expect has far reaching repercussions. Insofar as we depend on the tightly coupled technical systems of library operations, on batch processing, mechanical correction, upgrading and overlaying, copy-cataloging and shared databases, we are not free to do as we please. A failure to supply the system's requirements at any point destroys the system's reliability and its efficiencies. Non-cooperation, the rejection of agreed upon standards, and any other retreat from what the technical system requires for its successful operation means nothing less than the breakdown of the system, the introduction and proliferation of inefficiencies, inadequacies and failures.

Most American libraries (and many others elsewhere) are now totally dependent upon the proper functioning of the technical system. The requisite variety that regulation presupposes no longer resides in the library, but is dispersed among the contributors to a shared database, metadata vendors, and a system of outsourcing agencies. If anything goes wrong along the line, those at the end of the chain will never know. Furthermore many librarians and library administrators assume that the technical system by itself will provide for all of their needs and *therefore* they can exploit the system while being free from its demands. And the system *will* continue to turn out its product. So long as we refuse to look at the results, everything will appear to run smoothly. After all, it is largely the library users who will be forced to deal with the results, not library administrators.

Is it possible for any library to act responsibly *and* freely while participating in the tightly integrated system of bibliographic information sharing we use and trust in today? It is, and these papers were written to argue exactly how that is possible and what it means. To summarize these three papers, the argument is that it is possible for libraries to actually serve their users and freely choose to adopt or refrain from adopting the structures, standards, technologies and commitments at our disposal because it is the human intelligence which goes into the creation of a database that makes it intelligible and useful. The price of this freedom is that we can never blindly trust the technical system but must use it intelligently, critically and with discretion, always keeping in mind the library's users and the institution's purposes. Yet if one library—such as the Library of Congress—acts freely in relation to the technical system, whether or not the assumptions and logic informing those actions are intelligent, critical or valid, then every other library will also have to treat the technical system critically and with a clear understanding of its inadequacies and failures *since this local act of freedom destroys the reliability of the system*. To refuse to acknowledge that is "to cast our responsibility to the winds, and to find it coming back seated on the whirlwind."

The first paper printed here was originally written at the request of Jeffrey Beall for a special issue of *Cataloging & Classification Quarterly*. The length of the article, and my desire to get it published earlier than the timetable Jeffrey gave me, led me to withdraw it and seek to publish it elsewhere. In order to get these arguments out in time for the meetings of the Library of Congress Working Group on the Future of Bibliographic Control, and because I wanted to give it to my wife as a birthday present, I took the original version to a local bookbinder and had 12 copies printed, giving them to my wife and a few other persons who had influenced my work.

The second paper printed in this collection was my public response to the LC series decision. It was actually a summary of my 2004 monograph *The Theory and Practice of Bibliographic Failure*. It was not easy to condense 385 pages into four, but it will be a lot easier to read that four page letter rather than the monograph.

The final paper was read before the Second Meeting of the Library of Congress Working Group on the Future of Bibliographic Control, May 9th 2007 in Chicago. I have made a few small changes and included the printouts that were handed out at the meeting but were not available in the version on the Working Group's website. Of this paper Diane Hillman remarked on Litablog, May 9th 2007

> its ideas were not effectively presented, and whatever germ of usefulness contained therein was tainted by the inability of the author to understand the realities of how technology has changed our environment. This was a deeply 'conservative' (in the classic sense) screed, delivered by a rather improbable Don Quixote (in t-shirt and beret). But the windmill he tilts at is whirring madly, and he is unequal to the task of stopping it.

The windmill is indeed whirring madly. Just like a whirlwind, it seems.

David Bade
Joseph Regenstein Library
University of Chicago
6:15 AM, 4 September 2007

Politics and Policies for Database Qualities

For Thursday's Water Lily
Happy Birthday
October 11, 2006

Revised 2007

Acknowledgements

The bibliography attached to this work is itself a record of intellectual debts, but there are some to whom more acknowledgements are due. The extent of my debts to Roy Harris and Erik Hollnagel will be immediately obvious to anyone familiar with their works. Jeffrey Beall deserves special mention as it was he who asked me to write something on "data quality in bibliographic databases" and thus the idea for this paper was born. Particular thanks are also due to those who read and commented on earlier drafts of this paper: Charles Blair, Helen Buehler, Leigh Estabrook, Barry Hinman, Uwe Jochum, Don Krummel, Kathryn La Barre, Thomas Mann, Paul Marty, Mary Mastraccio, Wojciech Siemaszkiewicz and Pat Williams. And thank you, Neil Roberts, for the magnificent Frederick Douglass.

Abstract

The distinction between qualities inherent in things and qualities dependent upon the observer which was famously set forth by Galileo has led many to disregard the latter as "merely subjective," while others have understood that such qualities are often political matters connected to goals, purposes and values. Since the goals of different libraries differ as widely as their users, one can only investigate the quality of library catalogues in respect to specific user goals and purposes. Bibliographic databases and library catalogues are created and maintained according to policies carried out within organizational structures, and both of these factors have far reaching influence on how those databases and catalogues can be successfully used for the satisfaction of the diverse goals of its users. Library policies and organizational structures are examined in light of the literature on cognitive systems engineering, human error and High Reliability Organizations. The conclusion is that many current library work structures and policies exhibit conflicting goals, insufficient awareness of the risks involved, failure to treat the larger system (e.g. cooperative databases and networks) as a system, little or no attention to error, and a belief in technological solutions without any corresponding understanding of the requirements for successful implementation of technologies in real-world contexts.

Contents

I. The Realm of Quality
Galileo's Primary and Secondary Qualities
Qualitative Foundations of Quantitative Research

II. Purposes, Goals, Objectives
What are Libraries For?
What are Bibliographic Databases and Library Catalogues For?

III. Databases as Objects of Policy
Tasks, Tools and the Logic of Failure
Conflicting Goals and Library Policies
Policies that Court Failure
The Role of Organizational Structures in Quality Control
A Case Study: Classification on Receipt
Where Does Information Come From? Trust and Reliability as the Foundation of Database Quality

IV. Policy and Politics

V. Conclusion

VI. Bibliography

I. The Realm of Quality

Database quality, catalogue quality, information quality: Do these matter? Fernández-Molina noted that if one considers "information as something vital it follows that its absence, incompleteness, falsity or poor quality can produce real damage for the one who depends on it" (Fernández-Molina, 1995, p.320). An article in the *Wall Street Journal* concerning the effect on business of "junk" in databases was discussed in Wand and Wang (1996):

> Poor data quality can have a severe impact on the overall effectiveness of an organization. A leading computer industry information service firm indicated that it "expects most business process reengineering initiatives to fail through lack of attention to data quality." An industry executive report noted that more than 60% of surveyed firms (500 medium-size corporations with annual sales of more than $20 million) had problems with data quality. The *Wall Street Journal* also reported that, "Thanks to computers, huge databases brimming with information are at out fingertips, just waiting to be tapped. ... Just one problem: Those huge databases may be full of junk ... In a world where people are moving to total quality management, one of the critical areas is data." (p.86-87).

Not quite a decade later "high-quality data has emerged as a new basis for competition" and "analyzing leading data quality practice is a must" according to Lee (2004, p. 94).

During the interval between Wand and Wang (1996) and Lee (2004), the problem of information and database quality in the changing environment of information technologies was the topic of a number of papers by Naumann, who argued in 1999 that developments in information technology, instead of alleviating problems of database quality will exasperate them, that "demands for high quality information will increase" *because* of technological developments (Naumann and Rolker, 1999).

The development of computer networks has shifted much information seeking from individual databases to the open WWW and its multitude of autonomous data sources, and while the benefits and enlargment of capabilities that followed from this development were immediately celebrated, the problems created and exasperated by this same development have been largely ignored or passed over apparently on the misguided assumption that further technical developments will solve current problems without creating further trouble. It was a clear understanding of the problems created by technological developments that led Nauman to claim that "Low information quality is one of the most pressing problems for consumers of information integrated from autonomous sources" (Naumann, 2002, p.29). He described the problems associated with systems integrating information from multiple autonomous sources thus:

> Completeness and correctness in a DBMS [database management system] are defined with regard to the content of the underlying database. The assumptions toward this database are that it contains only correct data, and that it contains all relevant data (closed world assumption). ... Of course, DBMSs may also contain incorrect data; of course DBMSs may also not have all available data. However, compared to Web data sources, the owner of a DBMS has the power to change this situation. If there are inaccurate data, one can correct them, if data is missing, one can insert it. If the overall quality of the system is low, one can take measures to increase the quality aspects that are amiss. Web data sources on the other hand are autonomous. If completeness and correctness or the overall information quality is not satisfying, there is usually nothing the integrating system can do about it. (Naumann, 2001, p.5-6)

Independently Nord, Nord and Xu also argued that information quality is a growing problem precisely because of advances in information technology:

> More and more electronically captured information requires processing, storage, and distribution through information systems (Siau et al., 2001). ... Real-world practice suggests that D[ata]Q[uality] problems are becoming increasingly prevalent (Huang, Lee & Wang, 1999; Redman, 1998; Wang & Wang, 1996). The traditional focus on the input and recording of data needs to be offset with recognition that the systems themselves may affect the quality of data (Fedorowicz & Lee, 1998). IT advances can sometimes create problems rather than benefit the organization, if DQ issues have not been addressed properly. (Nord, Nord & Xu, 2005)

Some of the chief problems of searching across autonomous data sources are associated with metadata translation and interoperability. In a 2003 study of Dublin Core (DC) records Godby, Smith and Childress stated that "Without extensive human-mediated correction, or training that promotes more consistent application of the Dublin Core element semantics when the records are created, even the goal of limited interoperability is compromised." (2003, p. 8) Discussing linguistic aspects of semantic interoperability across user communities Jung-ran Park demonstrated the importance of metadata quality for searching digital image collections, noting that

> successful resource discovery and exchange across digital collections demands semantic interoperability of concept representation based on unambiguous, consistent and accurate resource description. Absent accurate mapping of cataloger-defined natural vocabularies onto DC metadata elements, semantic interoperability, even among digital collections employing the identical metadata scheme and digital collection management software configuration, will become increasingly problematic, leading to a decrement in information sharing. (Park, 2006, p.26)

Finally we note that in the wake of 9/11 information quality became an urgent matter apart from any consideration of technologies:

> Information Quality Management is critical for national security not just because of the myriad information types, including textual, audio, video and other complex information types and to the difficulties in collecting intelligence information, but because of the consequences of failure of national security caused by low-quality information. ... The collection of intelligence information requires rigorous procedures and technologies to error-proof the collection processes, to assure information quality and techniques for analyzing less-than-optimum-quality information. (English, 2005, p.18)

So apparently information quality matters—at least to some—and matters for different persons and for a variety of reasons, but what is "quality"? Woźniak (2002) remarked that quality is one of the oldest philosophical categories, a topic in western philosophy since Plato, and offered as a working definition of quality "the degree to which something fulfills given expectations" (p. 17). Pinto Molina (1998) argued that the modern understanding of quality as a *problem* is associated with industrial products and the break between producers and consumers created by the industrial revolution:

> We can locate the origin of the problem of quality—at least as we understand it today—in the industrial revolution. The direct relation between producer and consumer having disappeared, the consumer was transformed into a being incapable of influencing either the forms of his needs or his expectations. In broad strokes (though not to be interpreted simplisticly) we can say that the systems of quality came to restore or reconstruct the bridge between producers

and consumers in a mass society in which individual autonomy was diminished. (p. 171)

In an industrial mode of production, quantity of goods is the overriding concern and quality can only be located within the object itself since there are no particular users, uses or contexts of use: there are only mass produced objects hopefully indistinguishable one from the other, and all bound for a market. Yet like libraries, industries cannot ignore the users, and hence the institution of industry standards.

Domanovszky insisted that the work of the librarian "will be very bad if it attends only to the rules and not to the one for whom the rules were meant to serve" (quoted in Pogányné, 1999), yet to arrive at an understanding of quality which includes production, product and end user has proven to be a very difficult task. In a review and criticism of the notion of quality as it is found in the literature of information science, Paim, Nehmy and Guimarães (1996) described the theoretically confused (i.e. impossible) situation of the modern information scientist:

> Absolutizing the user can lead to the renunciation of the search for rigor and exactitude of information, and in the end to the renunciation of intrinsic attributes resulting in an exacerbated and chaotic relativism which, taken to the extreme implies attention to every desire of the user. On the other hand, attending exclusively to intrinsic attributes can lead to the growth of information systems or services alienated from the interests of the users, compromising its efficacy. ... In the current situation the information professional adopts the pretence of a neutral stance between these two poles: the truth of the information and the desire of the user. (p. 117-118)

Two years later Nehmy and Paim (1998) concluded with the comment that these two approaches—intrinsic excellence without reference to users, purposes and contexts on the one hand, and users' desires/needs on the other—are equally unsatisfactory from a theoretical point of view. Unfortunately, the excellent discussion in these two papers reveal the unsatisfactory state of affairs but leave us still within that sorry state.

Woźniak's definition has a hole in it: the subject of "given expectations." We do have "something" which fulfills expectations, but not an expector; Douglas and Ney's (1998) "missing persons" are still missing. It is this missing person who can bring together Nehmy and Paim's two unhappy lovers, Truth and Desire. Commenting on the major difference between the definition of quality in ISO 8402 and its replacement six years later (ISO 9000), Guerrini (2002) noted that "Compared to the past the satisfaction of the client assumes a greater importance in the definition of quality" (p. 17-18): in the former, quality is "in the properties and characteristics of a product or service which confers on it the capacity for satisfying expressed or implied needs" while the latter standard contains eight principles, the first of which is "orientation towards the client."[1]

Keeping Plato and the industrial revolution in mind, let us consider a working definition of quality that makes explicit the role of the agent and the agent's purpose(s): "a judgement by a particular agent that something is satisfactory to that agent for accomplishing a certain purpose." This leaves most every aspect of quality to be determined by the agents, given a particular situation and context, but the definition requires an agent with a purpose, an agent who will be able to determine what is satisfactory and what is not. What are the implications of defining quality as a social judgement? Of having an (unspecified) agent and an (unspecified) purpose in the definition of quality?

Galileo's Primary and Secondary Qualities

In 17th century Europe the problem of scientific communication (in the broadest meaning of that phrase) gave rise to numerous philosophical grammars and universal languages, theorized, invented and offered to the scientific community as essential tools for arriving at a true understanding and representation of nature. At the same time, from Galileo's *Saggiatore* of 1623 to Newton's *Philosophiae Naturalis Principia Mathematica* of 1687, mathematics was held to be the language of Nature herself:

> Philosophy is written in this grand book—I mean the universe—which stands continually open to our gaze, but it cannot be understood unless one first learns to comprehend the language and interpret the characters in which it is written. It is written in the language of mathematics, and its characters are triangles, circles, and other geometrical figures... (Galileo, 1960 [1623], p.183-184)

---

[1] Guerrini (2002), p.17. I have translated from his text rather than from the standards themselves.

For Galileo, some qualities (primary qualities) could be measured and therefore had a substantial (i.e. material) reality, whereas others (secondary qualities) were "no more than mere names so far as pertains to the subject wherein they reside, and that they have their habitation only in the sensorium."(Galileo, 1960 [1623], p.309)

Following Galileo the subsequent history of qualities in the various sciences has largely been a series of attempts to measure particular qualities or the more abstract notion of quality itself and refusals to investigate any unquantifiable quality, with a growing body of arguments for qualitative research and qualitative models arising within science only in the late 20th century.[2] The study of quality—in business, literature, library service, bibliographical databases and most every other area—has had for its ideal formal or quantifiable criteria such as precision, recall, timeliness and accuracy. However the criteria are defined, language as representation and a correspondence theory of truth are assumed to validate the enterprise of identifying and counting their objective instantiations. Yet as measures of quality such criteria are never satisfactory since they sometimes matter and sometimes do not, they are sometimes in conflict and sometimes not (e.g. the great debates over precision vs. recall (Fugmann, 1994) and timeliness vs. completeness (Chauveinc, 1983; Thomas, 1996)) and sometimes simply irrelevant. In discussions of bibliographic databases many librarians and library administrators of the past decade have attempted to bring greater weight to one or another criteria of quality (Calhoun, 2006), but all attempts to define quality in terms of some criteria—measurable or not—fail for the very same reasons as the secondary qualities failed for Galileo: quality is a judgement made by people, not a "thing" found in nature. We can measure time; we cannot measure timeliness. We can count how many bytes of information

---

[2] "The distinction between qualitative and quantitative models is not about the use of numbers; both types of models can be numerical. Rather it is a distinction resting on degrees of appoximation and idealization. Qualitative models contain more approximations and are more highly idealized than quantitative models. ... Qualitative models of molecular structure are rarely able to make highly accurate predictions about molecular geometry; however, they are thought to explain why molecules have the shapes that they do." (Weisberg, 2004, p.1071-1072). According to Weisberg qualitative theorizing is "a model-building norm that associates explanatory depth with the sacrifice of precision." (p. 1080).

in a bibliographical record, but since the amount of information one could enter into a record has no limit (cf. Blair, 1990), "completeness" cannot be measured.[3]

When surrogates for quality are selected, they are selected from an infinite set of possibilities and this selection itself rests on qualitative considerations, a judgement about what is important.[4] Even accepting some surrogate for measurement, no measurement can ever be exact. The required precision of measurement is always determined by the question, the purpose of measurement: How many miles to Erdene Zuu? may be answered in miles or kilometers but in human contexts never in millimeters or light years, and the width of a benzine molecule will never be given in inches or kilometers.[5] Unfortunately some writers have taken the further and unwarranted step of insisting that quality, when unquantifiable, is a purely subjective matter rather than a political and social matter of tremendous importance to the persons involved in a particular activity. Once the matter under discussion has been described as subjective there can be no further scientific debate but only an endless difference of opinions.[6] If quality in databases were a purely subjective matter (one person's timeliness is another person's tardiness, one person's precision is another person's mass of irrelevancies) then, like Galileo, we should simply banish discussions of quality from our professional meetings and publications.

---

[3] Of course, given standards for required elements and time in the queue, both timeliness and completeness *according to those standards* can be measured.

[4] A brief but excellent discussion of the role of qualitative considerations in the construction of quantitative models may be found in Hollnagel (1993, ch. 3).

[5] Lévy-Leblond (1996) pushes such reflections further, noting that all scientific statements are true only under certain conditions: it is only in the special conditions of a vacuum subject to gravity that all objects fall at the same rate; under normal conditions, it *is* true that iron and feathers fall at different rates of speed.

[6] Cf. Svagelski-Liassine (1990, p. 833) on error in science: "One cannot dissociate the problem of error from the problem of science, that is to say, from the advent of a discourse unifying minds in a community through a method according to which they understand one another. If this single discourse which establishes the norm for thinking in any given period does not exist, we remain on the level of a difference of opinion where anything goes: in order for there to be falsehood, one must posit something as true. The general perspective on the problem of error is therefore that of the possibility of science."

In large part this has happened, but for entirely other reasons.[7] One reason, an important one, was given by Armstrong (1994): "Coming late to the concept of quality—as we do in the information industry" (p. 30). Information systems have not been designed to evaluate the data input; they work well principally because that task is assumed to be done before the point of data entry.[8] Information technologies have extraordinary speed and power precisely because they do not distinguish between information and misinformation. (If they had to do that, they would not yet exist.) For system designers, system quality matters but data quality does not—that is a problem for the creators and users of particular databases. However, following certain users' needs and ignoring others, developments in information technologies have led to the most important change in the debates on database quality. That has not involved changing the choice of criteria for data quality but changing the focus from the *criteria* of quality to the *object* of quality: no longer the quality of information but the qual-

---

[7] The rage for TQM (Total Quality Management) and "quality circles" brought issues of quality to the literature, and to some extent continue to do so though only as management strategies with "users" in mind. Weick & Sutcliffe (2001, p.82) noted that TQM programs usually fail because of "organizational designs that focus on efficiency, success, homogeneity, and certainty rather than on inefficiency, failure, diversity, and surprise." In libraries at least, TQM does not seem to have led to any increased concern for the creation of information, much less its accuracy and the skills needed for this work. With few exceptions, only the user's need for timely access has been stressed. Outside the Anglo-American world one can find a much greater and more persistent interest in issues of quality, though much of this largely follows the TQM literature. See e.g. Wormell (1990), Freon (1996), Guía (1998), papers in the first 1998 issue of *Bulletin des bibliothèques de France* under the rubrique La démarche qualité (especially the paper by Mayère and Muet), Di Domenico (1999), Derfert-Wolf and Bednarek-Michalska (2000), Foglieni (2001), Berger and Kempf (2001), Guerrini (2002) and Zybert (2004).

[8] Patrick and Black (1964, p.29) stated this clearly in 1963: "Therefore we will assume that an acceptable scheme does exist for the subject analysis of library materials. The scheme may be implemented, as it is now, by human beings, or it may be computer based. In either event, we assume that the document is indexed according to some classification and/or subject heading scheme, and that the depth of such indexing is as great as resources allow." It should also be noted that they refuse to take into account promising developments in laboratories, preferring instead to base their discussion on the actual systems available.

ity of the searching system. Many have dropped all concerns about the quality of bibliographic description and focused their attention on the quality of the searching system, transforming "the theory of bibliographic description into a theory of bibliographical searching" (Svenonius, 2000, p.66). The quality of information technologies which exploit digital objects—whether those objects consist of metadata, full texts, non-textual objects or a combination of all of these—is now investigated, and the performance of such technical systems can easily—if not always meaningfully—be quantified. Yet there remain many good reasons for believing that, however much the searching system matters, the information available for searching—whether one calls that a catalogue, bibliographic database, embedded metadata or anything else—still matters, no less than and perhaps even more than in much older systems of abstracting, indexing and cataloging.

Qualitative Foundations of Quantitative Research

The avoidance of evaluating quality otherwise than quantitatively (measuring surrogates, criteria which are presumed to reliably indicate quality) is not an accidental characteristic of the history of science: it is inextricably connected to the epistemological, aesthetic, ethical and political values, beliefs and commitments which in fact underwrite science. Qualities which cannot be measured have no place in that science founded by Galileo and his contemporaries. Fortunately, theirs is not the only science, and current research acknowledges the necessity of studying and debating the qualitative dimensions of many subjects of human importance, not only in industry (as revealed in the ISO standards mentioned above), but in areas such as risk perception, news reports, human rights, working environment and national security. Yet even in the presence of that recognition quantitative methods predominate and the literature on database quality reflects this state of affairs: definitions of quality are offered, almost always in terms of a set of criteria (some essential, some merely desirable to some users), which are then used as surrogates for quality and can be counted, statistically treated and offered up as reliable indicators of quality. Any definition of quality relying on criteria requires assent to the criteria offered or it will have no persuasive power (authority) or validity for those who dissent in the identification and evaluation of the given criteria. Thus, some librarians insist on accuracy and completeness even in the face of backlogs while others insist on timeliness even in the face of mountains of useless nonsense. Those debates on criteria may be philosophically or empirically motivated but regardless of and independent of such motivations they always have political implications (Nehmy and Paim, 1998; Paim, Nehmy and Guimarães, 1996; Balaban, 1998).

Van Fraassen (2004) argued that "flouting the criteria" is "at times" (some would say often) a prerequisite for scientific progress:

> Science is a representation of nature, in mathematical form, accomplishing by this means ... *a certain end* that philosophers debate. Criteria of success or completeness for scientific representation must be related to this end, but appear concretely in science itself in theory choice and evaluation. Remarkably, scientific progress at times involves precisely the rejection of previously proclaimed criteria." (p. 794; ellipsis and italics in original).

Hollnagel (1993) commented on the paradox that "in order to have quantification it is necessary first to have a proper qualitative description or model. In other words, it is necessary to specify the data that are needed before they can be sought." (p. xx) These remarks by van Fraassen and Hollnagel refer to a paradox rooted in the temporal and political existence of human beings and that project we call science: qualitative descriptions are necessary for any object of study, but the history of science is the history of the successive abandonment (or, more charitably, the refinement) of those qualitative descriptions. For present purposes what is important is the recognition that it is these qualitative descriptions (presuppositions, commitments, models, goals) that *must* underwrite and inform any discussion of quality in databases, library catalogues or services (e.g. the differences between the ISO standards mentioned above). There can be no objective evaluation of quality separated from particular users and particular contexts for everything depends on who you ask and what you want.[9] In brief: *quality* is not a theoretical term at all, but a term indicative of a social judgement, much like *information*.

The recognition that quality is not a thing in nature (or in a product) which can be studied in isolation but a judgement made by a particular person or group of persons at a particular time in a particular

---

[9] "When does a database have quality? The answer depends upon who asks the question, the knowledge of the person evaluating the database and its records, and the use of the electronic information." (Arnold, 1992, p.38)

context, rooted in particular values and commitments means that all discussions of quality must arise either within the context of shared goals and commitments—perhaps explicitly formulated in a constitution, oath or mission statement—or in debates over what those goals and commitments (constitutions, oaths, mission statements) are or should be. The importance of such debates has been central to recent work in economics:

> From that commonly adopted perspective qualities are intrinsic characteristics of the products to which they are attached and from which they are inseparable. The consumers are supposed to perceive these qualities (and therefore the importance of information) and the hypothesis is made that the way in which they perceive, evaluate and classify them depends on their own preferences. They can be considered as strictly individual (as in the standard neoclassical model) or (as in the extreme sociological version) linked to their membership in a group or social class ... In the perspective that we adopt, this separation is impossible: the qualities of a product depend on the joint work of a combination of actors and there is no reason to think that the consumers do not participate in the determination of quality any less than the other actors. (Callon, Meadel and Rabeharisoa, 2000, p.223-224)

Whether the product is material or mental, activity or goal, the decisions made at the planning stage (design, policies and organizational structures) and the assumptions about quality which inform them can be far more important for the final product and its evaluation by the end users than the efforts of those who actually produce the product (those at the "sharp end"). Far from being "merely subjective" debates unworthy of scientific interest, debates concerning quality are the very debates which define what the product (science, scholarship, research, professionalism, libraries, databases) should be, not merely what these may be here and now. Accordingly, every discussion of quality in bibliographic databases must either assume a certain qualitative understanding of databases or engage in a debate about just what a database should be, its purposes, goals, objectives and the activities that it should support. Which is where we shall begin.

II. Purposes, Goals, Objectives

> If every public organization's reason for being is to achieve the goals assigned to it, then every orientation, every option, every procedure

should logically be evaluated solely in regard to the result and the effects which they produce.

Although this seems to be good sense, everyone knows that it is far from a reflection of reality. (Giappiconi, 2001, p. 15)

A growing body of literature on industrial accidents (e.g. Reason, 1995), planning disasters (Dörner, 1997; Morel, 2003), business failures (Kerdellant, 2000) and high reliability organizations (Rochlin, et al., 1987) has identified an unclear understanding of goals, conflicting goals and decisions radically contrary to the organizational goals as primary sources of catastrophic failures, disasters, accidents and all manner of undesirable outcomes; undesirable outcomes, it should be noted, from the perspective of the goals clearly formed beforehand or acknowledged in hindsight. If we accept this lesson we can begin the study of quality in bibliographic databases with inquiries into the purposes and goals of bibliographic databases, situating that inquiry within the organizational context of a library. What are libraries for? What users and uses do bibliographic databases serve?

What are Libraries For?

Discussions of the quality of bibliographic databases and library catalogues presupposes not only their existence but also reasons for their existence, the validity of those reasons and the utility or value of their continued existence. One of the directions characterizing much of the literature on the future of libraries published in the 1990's and the first decade of the 21st century is a desire to reorient the purposes, objectives and goals of libraries to bring them in line with a certain state of affairs (economic, technical and social), whether that is deemed to be a current, imminent or inevitable state of affairs. The library literature of the past decade has been full of references to "virtual libraries," predictions of the end ("access to full-text will render all work on MARC useless" Melot (1993, p.10) declared), and discussion of the "Death and transfiguration of catalogues" (special section of the *Bulletin des bibliothèques de France*), the "library as portal to the Internet" (Thomas, 2000), "The assassination of the catalogers" (Revelli, 2004), questions such as "Must we burn libraries?" (Keriguy and Dalhoumi, 1991), and even "Can we move the librarian *into* the databank?" (Chauvin and Papy, 2005). It is significant that the redefinition of the purposes and goals of libraries, the roles of librarians, and the needs and desires of library users has been articulated, argued and advocated largely by library administrative personnel on the grounds of cost-benefit analyses rather than by front-line library practitioners (reference librarians, bibliographers). It is also significant that these calls for radical change are both motivated by and oriented toward technological developments and the beliefs which accompany them.[10] Most importantly, and in spite of claims to the contrary, the changing ideas about what libraries are and what they should be have *not* been forced upon librarians by economic realities or technological developments, neither have they been demanded by politicians, nor by library users. Debates concerning the nature of libraries, their purposes and goals, have been and continue to be debates within the community of librarians about who we are, what we do, and why. Our appreciation of the quality of libraries, library catalogues and librarians depends entirely upon how we answer these questions. In the absence of any agreement on what we do, for whom and why, we cannot arrive at any consensus on the purpose of and hence the quality of bibliographic databases and library catalogues.

If evaluation of the quality of databases depends upon the purposes and goals of the users of the database, then one might assume that in order to construct a quality database creators of databases must have a clear and accurate understanding of the purposes and goals of the database users. Yet such knowledge is impossible to obtain in the vast majority of cases (e.g. public libraries, academic libraries) since these institutions are built not for a homogenous, stable and known community of predictable users—for current residents, students, faculty and staff—but for these *and* unknown and unknowable groups of future users and their uses. "The user resists that rationalization, representing herself everyday in a new and unpredictable fashion" Galli (2001, p.239) insisted, making user models suspect if not downright misleading.[11] It is of course possible to survey current users and to

---

[10] On the cultural accompaniment of technologies, I have found especially interesting the numerous works of Gilbert Hottois, Philippe Breton, Wanda Orlikowski and Uwe Jochum.

[11] "Technically, the problem is often expressed as a question of identifying user needs and preferences, with suggestions that the problem is solved by finding or having the right user model. ... The concept of a user model is, however, close to being conceptually vacuous ... User models are not a viable

predict all manner of futures, but surveys of current users have only indicated the vast range of uses and can no more serve to define future use patterns than technological prognosticators can predict future technologies, much less the uses that will be made of them. If neither the Man-on-the-Street nor Nostradamus are useful guides for determining the needs of database users, are there any other sources outside the library for obtaining acceptable descriptions of the user goals which ought to ground and orient the library's self-understanding and mission? Or are we truly free to invent, manipulate, ignore or discard actual users and future responsibilities by simply declaring that our current situation or some imagined scenario is the one and only desirable possibility for libraries?

For many libraries, such externally generated purposes have been provided. The Library of Congress is one example: that library was explicitly founded to serve the needs of the United States Congress (which institution was itself explicitly founded to serve the people of the United States) whatever those needs may be now or in the future. In the *Final Report* of the Provost's Task Force on the University Library, completed in 2006, the Joseph Regenstein Library of the University of Chicago received a mandate from the university of which it is a part. In that report we find the first Particular Principle for guiding the future of the Regenstein Library:

> The main purpose of Regenstein is research and should remain research. There are a variety of aspects to this principle. It means we feel that heavy users should continue to be the highest priority in service, and it is their research success we should be aiming to facilitate. Also, it means that the library's public spaces should celebrate the research function and that the University should work harder to expose its undergraduates to library research as one of the forms of knowledge generation. We also feel that the library should start to recognize that it will increasingly have a constituency beyond University of Chicago users. As other major libraries remove research materials to offsite storage, Regenstein will become more and more attractive to colleagues elsewhere. In some senses, the Trustees have already envisioned the library as a facility whose research constituency will reach well beyond the University of Chicago. We recog-

---

solution as variability within and between situations and users is too large." (Hollnagel & Woods, 2005, p.85) nize that judgment and applaud it.¹² (University of Chicago, Provost's Task Force on the University Library, 2006)

The choice of focus (purpose) is crucial since focusing upon maximum demands (service to the heaviest users) ensures that minimum demands (service to casual users) can be met, whether this entails user education or the development of alternate system interfaces (e.g. searching LCSH subjects as keywords and as exact sequences; short, long and MARC displays in online catalogues).¹³ How institutional policies and organizational structures can render the best technologies ineffective simply by failing to plan for the maximum demands is highlighted in Hollnagel and Woods' (2005) observation that in many organizations

> tasks are designed so that the minimum demands require maximum capacity. This means that humans are supplemented—or replaced—by automation to ensure that the task can be accomplished under optimal conditions of work. What should rather be done is to design tasks so that the maximum demands can be met by the normal capacity—or preferably even by the minimum capacity. ... The main concern is not the temporary level of efficiency (or safety), but rather the ability of the system to sustain acceptable performance under a variety of conditions. (p. 123-124)

---

[12] Compare the University of Chicago report with those released by the University of California Libraries, Bibliographic Services Task Force (2005), Indiana University (Byrd, et. al, 2006) and the LC report (Calhoun, 2006).

[13] Opposite the sophisticated user are what Hollnagel and Woods call the "accidental users", users who have to use the library rather than wanting to. The importance of the "accidental user" for the design of systems and the challenges they present are as different as their use is from the "heaviest users" identified by the University of Chicago task force: "The spread of information ... means that there are many situations where users interact with information technology artefacts because they *have* to rather than because they *want* to. The possibility of doing something in another, more conventional—and presumably familiar—way has simply disappeared. Examples include finding a book in a library, ... The accidental user poses a particular challenge to the design of artefacts because most of the relevant disciplines ... are predicated on the assumption that users are motivated and have the required level of knowledge and skills. ... [T]he accidental user should be considered as if governed by a version of Murphy's Law, such as: 'Everything that can be done wrongly, will be done wrongly.'" (Hollnagel and Woods, 2005, p. 109-110)

Other libraries, such as those established by religious organizations, literacy programs, law firms and scientific institutions, have been created to serve particular and usually well-defined and widely known social objectives. In such institutions the goal of the library is to educate the user according to a particular set of goals articulated in the larger social institutions which have established the libraries; in the examples above this would entail educating the users in the ways of religion, reading, law and science respectively.

The relationship of the library (and therefore librarians) to its users thus cannot merely be one of slavishly following the whims of whoever enters the library or uses its website but rather a relationship grounded in certain social goals and objectives defined and mandated by the social institution to which it is answerable, whether synagogue, school, law firm, township or NGO. In the words of Accarisi "The librarian cannot simply be carried away on the indiscriminate wave of the desires of the users anymore than by some theoretical model of system quality not intelligently adapted to the library and its functions. On the contrary, she must be the interpreter ... of the function and mission of her library." (Jahier & Accarisi, 2001, p.238). The purpose of each library is therefore first of all and above all to serve the particular users of a particular community—whether that is a locally established community, an international group or a "virtual" community of strangers—in their actions towards an established goal. Since these goals have their origins in practices existing prior to and beyond the library, their fulfillment requires understanding these practices and their requirements.

Can an art historian develop and evaluate a library for a law firm (and vice versa)? Can a rabbi do this for a fundamentalist Christian seminary (and vice versa)? Can a musician who cannot read music adequately build and maintain a sheet music collection for music historians? The answer in all cases is: Yes, provided they first acquire an intimate knowledge of the languages and practices of the communities whom they serve; otherwise, the answer must be No. Commenting on Wittgenstein's remark "If a lion could talk we could not understand him," Blair (2003) wrote as follows:

> The reason we could not understand the speaking lion is that we have no personal experience of the activities in which he is engaged. If we can come to understand the meaning of a word by looking at its use, then meaning is intimately linked to the activities and practices that we have in common with others. If we do not have any ac-

tivities in common, then there is nothing that we can talk about. (p.16)

If Wittgenstein (and Blair and a host of other philosophers and linguists) are correct, then one essential prerequisite for successful (read: quality) libraries would be that librarians and library users have certain activities in common. The goals of the library being rooted in these common practices, both the librarians and the library users would evaluate the library on the same or similar assumptions concerning quality.

Local libraries and librarians working with local library users are already embedded in a context that enables them to communicate: the life of that community. Academic libraries do not (yet?) strive to supply hammers, coffee and internet chat service to everyone who wants to borrow hammers, drink coffee and search for love-on-line. What they (still?) strive to do is to make available specialized periodicals for the student of e.g. infectious diseases in the Ottoman Empire and the periodical indexes (whether printed or online) which can lead the student through the mass of potentially relevant literature. On the other hand, any library developed to serve the global information society (with anonymous librarians serving anonymous users) has no clearly defined user group, user context or mission. The vague and the universal do not permit qualitative assessment, nor concrete plans and actions—an important factor in planning and management failure noted by Dörner (1997).

In an era when librarians are constantly urged to update their goals and their activities, to make them reflective of and useful to a society imagined to be a global information society in which knowledge workers are (or ought to be) important, the focus on the purpose and goals of libraries and librarians is both salutary and crucial since diverse libraries serve diverse purposes and users. Research on sense making in libraries and other organizations, whether involving oral or written language, whether direct (face-to-face) or technologically mediated, nearly always concedes that meaning making is context dependent, that one cannot speak of the "same information" in different contexts. Therefore we should not be surprised that in the evaluation of libraries and databases, one librarian's mountain is another librarian's molehill. Everything depends on what the librarian hopes to do and to achieve with the library collection, its catalogue, and available databases.

What are Bibliographic Databases and Library Catalogues For?

Library catalogues and bibliographies have a long history, and the difficulties of maintaining and using these tools were a strong impetus in the development of information technologies; electronic bibliographic databases and catalogues were some of the first kinds of research tools converted to electronic forms. Their future, however, has become a matter of debate. Lupovici announced in 1996 the end of catalogues for electronic documents ("Aujourd'hui, avec le document électronique qui comporte en lui-même les données catalographiques, nous pouvons annoncer l'éradication du catalogage dans les bibliothèques pour tous les documents électroniques.") and Thomas (2000) suggested that the library catalogue should be a portal to a more important information source, the World Wide Web. Since her suggestion much has changed and now many of her colleagues at the Library of Congress and elsewhere are advocating—insisting!—that the information which was once available only in a particular library's catalogue should now be made available—along with every other information source in the world—*only* through the WWW via such search engines as Google. For librarians such as Marcum, Google should replace the library catalogue:

> But as we develop digital resources, the question arises—do we need to provide detailed cataloging information for these digitized materials? Or can we think of Google as the catalog? (Marcum, 2005, p. 6)

> If the commonly available books and journals are accessible online, should we consider the search engines the primary means of access to them?" (Marcum, 2005, p. 11).

Calhoun agrees, although she admits "catalog records will have a role to play in discovery and retrieval of the world's library collections for at least a couple of decades and probably longer." (Calhoun, 2006, p. 27)

If bibliographic databases such as library catalogues are to be replaced by Google searching or something else, then the matter of quality in library catalogues is a dead issue, or at least dying. The pressing issue for some librarians is therefore not so much the quality of bibliographic databases considered in themselves, but their capacity in comparison to a bibliographic universe absorbed into something like Google. To advocate the continued maintenance of autonomous library catalogues in 2006 requires an argument demonstrating that these do what Google (or Google's promises) cannot do, that local catalogues offer a qualitatively different information environment than Google does or can. By clarifying the goals of bibliographic research the different searching possibilities presented by Google and autonomous catalogues or bibliographic databases can be evaluated. In the interest of brevity I shall limit my remarks to a single context: the large academic research library, that being the type of institution in which I have spent most of my life.

Research in an academic library

We begin with a few remarks by Abbott (2006):

> There is very little serious social science written about the humanities or humanistic social sciences as research enterprises, and there is almost no serious writing by disciplinary social scientists about the library as a social or organizational form. There is a good deal of writing about libraries and library knowledge from an informational science (IS) standpoint, but the theory of knowledge it presupposes is rooted, like IS itself, in engineering-based theories of information that turn out to be largely irrelevant to what it is that humanistic research actually produces.

Abbott begins his sketch of a theory of library research with the statement "library research is research with records," and follows with a description of the contrast between the nature of library research and research in the natural sciences. The principal differences he locates "in their modes of research production," the latter being characterized by division of labour. His description of library research I quote at length:

> By contrast, records-based research is most often artisanal, the product of lone scholars who read a variety of primary records and secondary material, who if they code things at all code them idiosyncratically, and who in due time turn out publications that are seldom if ever exactly comparable with or precisely connected to prior work. There are of course exceptions, but in general the contrast between the natural sciences and records-based library research is quite strong.

From a computational point of view, natural science with its broadly-shared definitions and formal cumulation works rather like a structured program while records-based research—with its lone scholars turning idiosyncratic inputs into new outputs that then become others' new inputs—works like a neural net. The move that underlies this analogy is thinking about the architecture of each system as a whole rather than envisioning each as simply an aggregative sum of researchers' products. That is, I am not talking here about a model of a single investigator's or research team's mode of production, but rather about the entirety of library research or science taken as a whole.

Library research is, then, a fairly simple net computing system. Like most such net systems and indeed like most current optimization routines, library research relies heavily on browsing, which can be defined somewhat formally as random inspection of a local knowledge vicinity for items with a high probability of payoff, particularly in terms of taking one to productive new localities. It is crucial to recognize that this happens at many different levels in library research, not just at one: within books as one turns pages, on shelves as one searches for a book, in the stacks as one walks by unknown call numbers, in bibliographic indexes and other research tools as one glances through topics, and so on. In all these cases, the power of browsing is great. Note that this means that browsing is a constant concomitant of library research, not an occasional activity within it. Browsing is always going on and gaining knowledge from browsing is not a rare, serendipitous event but rather a constant, routine one.

Browsing has two requirements. First, the materials being browsed must already themselves be highly ordered either by virtue of their internal structure or by their places in an indexing or cataloguing or classification system. Otherwise, adjacency has no meaning and browsing can't work. Second, the browsers must have broad knowledge that primes them to recognize likely connections. This is the rationale for general exams, for example. (Note that by this argument, one can even think of conversation with other scholars as a form of mutual browsing.)

This insight provides us with a first reason why much of library technologization doesn't work very well. The assumption is that given "the right indexing system," you can replace the expert browser, and any college freshman will be able to write good scholarship. But this can't be true because such an indexing system would only work if it encoded the expertise of all the possible expert users. But in that case it would reproduce the confusion (of all the different possible associations to a given item) within itself, giving the novice no more guidance than the old tools. What technology usually offers, in fact, is the expertise of only one user—a hard-coded set of hyperlinks—which is obviously vastly impoverished from a computational point of view unless you can assume that there is one (or a few) right expert(s), which is seldom true in the areas that employ library research.

I emphasize browsing because such random search in pre-organized localities, although important in the natural sciences (it is after all Pasteur who said that chance favors only the prepared mind), is by no means as important as it is in library research. Library research as currently practiced is unthinkable without browsing. It is quite often the case that library researchers do not know exactly what they want ahead of time; indeed one might define skill at library research as the ability to recognize, when we have found something, that it is in fact something that we ought to have wanted to find. To be sure, library researchers are sometimes quite focused in their needs. But even during tasks like coding and focused retrieval, browsing goes on in the background. It is for this reason that artisanal researchers do not often subdivide their work and give brute force tasks to others; they worry about the loss of browsing.

Browsing in this extremely broad sense and at all these many levels is thus one thing that absolutely must be protected in the research libraries of the future. It means keeping materials ordered and in a setting where they can be effectively scanned in the random fashion that browsing demands. Since, as we have noted, browsing involves many levels of organization, all of these levels need to be preserved, not just the order of books on shelves. (Abbott, 2006)

The recognition of common practices such as browsing is crucial for understanding the goals of an academic research library. Academic research libraries have historically been quite different from other (e.g. government or commercial) research libraries in that they serve researchers who have been bound neither to research programs dictated by government demands and restrictions nor to the outcomes desired by stockholders or the dictates of the market.[14] The predict-

---

[14] That the situation in the post-World War II era has broken the boundaries between universities, governments and the market, entangled perhaps the

able result of this ideal of interest motivated and unfettered research is an unpredictable range of research, unpredictable results, and a strong leaning towards research in virgin territory where the literature has not been surveyed or even published. Research questions are not handed down from a corporate sponsor or government program but are usually formulated and refined in the course of the research itself.

One striking character of original research is the inadequacy of previous vocabularies, previous research and standard reference tools to direct or even describe the literature of interest: creating new fields of research requires new terminologies, new classifications and new tools. Yet the original researcher, not the librarian, creates those vocabularies, classifications and often the appropriate research tools themselves (e.g. bibliographies accompanying dissertations). Since the researcher does not (and cannot) expect the library to provide these services prior to his/her research, what can the researcher expect? There is no single answer to that question; the answers vary from researcher to researcher, from discipline to discipline and from institution to institution.

An important factor influencing what the researcher expects will be the depth of materials offered by the library: the student of Burmese or Javanese literature will find more and expect more in the way of primary sources and reference services at Northern Illinois University than at the University of Chicago whereas the reverse would be true for the historian of ancient India or for the physicist.[15] Another factor

---

majority of research (at least in some institutions such as MIT) with the demands, limitations and secrecy imposed by governments and industrial firms, and so far degraded the minds of many scientists and scholars that the pursuit of an unwelcome (e.g. unprofitable, politically undesirable) truth can be the object of scorn and even fought by lobbies in Congress does not require the abandonment of that prior ideal of science in the service of some greater good. Many of us who caught a glimpse of that ideal in our school days lament its repudiation by librarians, scientists and scholars in their rush to embrace the globalizing forces of capital, international government and sociotechnical integration of all under one law, that of technological progress in a global market.

[15] In this connection it is worth noting that an advocate of digital libraries has acknowledged that "the intellectual integrity of collections built and nurtured by knowledgeable individuals is a lasting tribute to the scholarly community. This is the function that may not be readily accommodated in a digital library." (Marcum, 1997)

is the library's participation in cooperative agreements and interlibrary loan networks: during my time at the University of Illinois at Urbana-Champaign there was literally nothing which I could not get from anywhere in the world so long as I had at least a partially correct citation and I or another librarian could locate a copy somewhere.[16] At other institutions, reciprocal borrowing and international borrowing or copying are restricted, costly or simply unavailable. Yet both of these factors—local availability, cooperative agreements—depend upon knowing that something exists, whether here or elsewhere. And there the literature search begins: what needs to be examined, what read, where can it be found and how obtained? Andrew Abbott's browser puts on his hiking boots and the hunt is on.

The academic library user and the catalogue

How do researchers know what they need or want to read and how do they find it? I shall offer one of a multitude of correct answers, based on my own experience. When inspired by or intrigued by something found in my reading I pursue the matter by looking for other books by the author or citations in the work I am reading. The more I read, the more my own ideas and plans take shape and the directions in which I need to proceed become clear and therefore searchable in a catalogue. I do not at any point want to locate "everything in the world" on the topic because even if that were possible, not everything is useful for scholarly purposes. It is of course impossible to recognize "everything" on a topic unless the topic is already completely known and its boundaries firmly established, i.e. only when there is nothing more that can be said or written. So long as it is possible to ask a question, the boundaries of the topic and therefore the relevant literature remain unknowable for the researcher and impossible for information technologies to identify.

In 1993 I had the opportunity of cataloging a Javanese dance-drama published in celebration of the 700th anniversary of the founding of the kingdom of Majapahit. The story is in large part the tale of a Javanese king in exile who was returned to his rightful position as king by the assistance of the Mongol army. No mongolist had ever written more than one paragraph on the topic, but this dance-drama

---

[16] The importance of catalogue quality for library cooperation broadly considered is briefly but excellently argued in Sapori (1995).

was unlike anything I had ever read in the standard treatments of Mongolian history. So I decided to study the Mongol invasion of Jawa, and for that I needed background materials on many matters about which I knew nothing: ship-building in China, Arab merchants and pirates in Southeast Asian waters, trade relations between the various political, military and commercial powers of the period, Balinese historiographical traditions, Old Javanese poetic genres, diplomatic protocols of the Mongols, and a multitude of other matters which were obviously not discussed or cited in the source materials or the dance-dramas and largely absent from what little literature directly related to the invasion I could locate. Where did I go? I went to the library and searched the catalogue and browsed the stacks for general histories and bibliographies on the Mongols, medieval Javanese history, Southeast Asian commerce, and so on. Finding these, I moved on to the citations found therein, following chains of references, searching in databases for authors who had written on the topics of interest and criticism of the source materials. New questions arising during the course of reading set the cycle of search and browsing in motion again and again. This strategy, not an uncommon one, is based on the need to find some point of entry into a large area of scholarship in hopes of finding therein a handful of items that identify sources, discuss the history of scholarship, provide context, eliminate incompatible interpretations and strengthen others, or lead to something more relevant. The library provides both the guidance and the materials for examination and study.

Others might perhaps go to Google—as I did later (see below)—using or citing any number of short histories that can be found, and be done with it. And in the library they can do that. The question is: Should libraries focus their technical systems and searching capacities on the common research practices of dilettantes or the "average" user, or should they seek to develop and instruct users in the best research strategies? How academic librarians answer that question will depend upon how they answer the question of what academic libraries are for, what research is, and what the role of the library in that process should be.

A number of recently published user studies have described the habits and desires of researchers as though the authors of these studies were in need of finding out what research was and how it is done by students and scholars.[17] The interpretation of these studies has varied widely, something which should be expected whenever researchers attempt to approach a normatively determined social practice objectively and refuse to recognize its essentially normative character. A recent and controversial use of those studies to support policies calling for the radical reorientation of library catalogues and restructuring of library practices involved in their creation and maintenance was commissioned by the Library of Congress and critiqued by a librarian of that same library (see Calhoun, 2006; Mann, 2006a). The assertions (there are no arguments) made in Calhoun (2006) reflect attitudes common among library managers and to simplify matters somewhat this interpretation of user studies may be summarized as asserting that today's library users do not use the catalogue and when they do it does not satisfy their needs.

While Mann (2005) has argued that Marcum and Calhoun have misinterpreted and distorted the findings of the user studies cited in their papers (and I concur with his assessment) it is still possible to pursue the question raised in Marcum's and Calhoun's papers without passing judgement on the value of their interpretations: what is the library catalogue for? The simple, traditional answer is that it is an inventory of the holdings of a particular library, designed to be searchable by authors, titles and, during the past century, subjects also. In the electronic catalogue it is possible to search any given field in the bibliographical record, provided, of course, that the information has been correctly and completely imput and correctly identified with the appropriate metadata. The catalogue is not, as Google aims to be, a guide to all the world's information.[18] This answer may be interpreted broadly to cover not only materials of all formats physically present in the library but materials available remotely from warehouses, cooperating institutions, freely available material on the Internet and restricted electronic resources available to local users on-line. The number of possible approaches to information about the library's

---

[17] For a review of that literature, see Mann (2005).
[18] For an interesting discussion of the role of libraries in the organization of "all the world's information" see Hjørland (2000). As a thought experiment we might consider what it would mean to claim to "organize all the world's information" if, like many philosophers, economists and biologists today, the price of tea in China, the temperature of a Hungarian newt's nose, your DNA and everything else are considered to be "information."

available resources will depend upon the design of the catalogue, both the technical system and the techniques of bibliographic description which inform the catalogue entries.

A qualitative contrast: Google and the Joseph Regenstein Library catalogue

Abbott (2006) stressed the point that "most of the technologies that today aim to automate or simplify or replace parts of library research do not in fact accomplish what it accomplishes now, but rather do something different to a greater or lesser extent," a point which he elaborated as follows:

> That we now can retrieve known sources extremely quickly is important only to the extent that retrieving known sources is an important or essential part of the research process. In fact, while focused retrieval is important, any library researcher knows that it is nowhere near as important as is figuring out what are the things that we want to retrieve in the first place. Or again, that everyone in the world may be able to have access on-line to every book in the University of Michigan Library via Google means nothing whatever unless that universal access helps rather than hinders the general process of library research that I have outlined above. But it is quite possible that the accessibility of huge amounts of hitherto unavailable material to unskilled researchers will in fact flood the scholarly system with so much bad work that its selection systems will break down, with the result that knowledge as a whole will actually be worsened by the new technological accessibilty.
>
> This fact reminds us that, despite the simplistic image of "speeding up scholarship," what matters about library research is how the overall system performs, not whether one researcher finds a particular source faster or slower. (Abbott, 2006)

The purpose and usefulness of the restricted focus of a library catalogue can be demonstrated easily. In May 2006 I searched Google for keywords *Mongol + Java* and *Mongols + Java*. The first search retrieved 326,000 results while the second retrieved 116,000 results. One month later the former search repeated retrieved 430,000 results. The same searches performed in the catalogue of the Joseph Regenstein Library produced two results, the only two non-fiction books ever published on the topic of the Mongol invasion of Jawa, neither of which appear in the first 200 results in the Google searches.

A search of these terms in OCLC at the same time produced 10 results including one of the items found in the Regenstein Library catalogue. A record for the second book is also in the OCLC database, but since it was supplied by a Japanese library with Japanese description (including subject headings) it cannot be retrieved by *any* search utilizing non-Japanese search terms. This problem, growing exponentially in OCLC because of international contributions, is beyond all human or mechanical means of control for Internet search engines such as Google. The reason that the Regenstein Library catalogue can not only retrieve both of these items but also only these two is simple: in the Regenstein Library a cataloger examined both books, created appropriate subject headings—headings which did not exist previously because of the non-existence of one book and the Japanese language record for the other—and added these records to the local catalogue.[19] We can press the matter further: the Japanese book is in a number of US libraries but in none of these had the heading *Java (Indonesia)--History--Mongol invasion, 1292-1293* been used because it had not been established in any subject thesaurus in use in those libraries. (The headings used were: *China--History--Yuan dynasty, 1280-1368. China--Relations--Java (Indonesia). Java (Indonesia)--Relations--China*, a reasonable set of subject headings given the subject of the book, but not one allowing access to a search using the terms *Mongol* and *Java*.)

If we follow Thomas (1996), we should interpret the quantitative difference between these two searches as revealing the overwhelming qualitative superiority of Google. On the other hand, according to David Bade the mongolist, these same numbers reveal the superior efficiency of the Regenstein Library catalogue. More importantly, these numbers reveal something else. The difference between the results in the Regenstein Library catalogue and Google reveals much about the differences between these two kinds of research tools and their goals. The former is a guide to just what is available in or through a particular institution and is therefore limited. For the researcher on medieval Jawa that limitation acts as a powerful tool since it means that even such a general search as *Mongol + Java* produces exact results, retrieving the only two books on the topic which would

---

[19] Because that cataloger—a certain David Bade—was not authorized to upgrade or contribute Japanese vernacular records to the OCLC database, no changes were made there and thus the discrepancy between the search results in OCLC and in the Regenstein library catalogue.

be relevant to a medievalist studying Javanese history or the Mongols, it indicates that both books are available here and now, and a look into those books reveals the most complete bibliography ever published devoted to the incidents of 1292-1293. The Regenstein Library catalogue demonstrates the intelligent organization of information for the specific purpose of scholarly research.

The Google results in contrast appear to be simply absurd. Why 162,000 for the plural form and 326,000 for the singular? Why 100,000 more items retrieved on the latter search one month later? The Google search right away presents the searcher with hate literature (hits for the UglyChinese.org website), nationalist propaganda, undocumented educational materials for high school students, dictionaries, encyclopedia entries that link to themselves in an endless chain of undocumented texts of unknown authorship and without other references, commercial information sources, marketing sites that have nothing to do with Jawa or the Mongols, and somewhere down there, we hope, citations to books by Niwa Tomosaburo and David Bade (full text being unavailable in either case, unless someone has stolen our books and copied them). The least valuable sources appear at the top of the hit list, the result of statistical relevance ranking without anything that could be mistaken for human judgement, while the important sources cannot be found in a reasonable amount of time.

The numerous calls for fast as opposed to accurate cataloging have been advocated by the very librarians who are now pushing to have Google replace the catalogue. Unfortunately, Google does not merely slow down research, it makes finding important material "virtually" impossible. In the presence of 430,000 items retrieved *ALL* access vanishes and neither timeliness nor accuracy are achieved. The reason that this mass of distracting, useless misinformation obscures and makes the retrieval of relevant material impossible (i.e. is an obstacle to research) is that the goal of Google is to "organize" *all* of the world's information. This, of course, includes all of the world's lies, misinformation and machine generated nonsense.[20] Statistical tools cannot evaluate information and distinguish it from nonsense much

---

[20] "We hear, in this dawn of the so-called information age, a great deal of talk about the explosion of information and the new methods for its dissemination. It is important to realize, however, that most of what is disseminated is misinformation, badly organized information or irrelevant information." (Gell-Mann, quoted in Heck (2001), p. 11)

less misinformation. A Google search can certainly produce "a" bibliography, but if one were to compile a bibliography on the Mongols Google style, it would be an absolutely useless bibliography.[21] The scholar's bibliography, even when it strives to be "the" bibliography of a given topic, is always limited by what the scholar judges to be worth referencing.[22]

The Catalogue as filter

A library catalogue is not *the* tool for bibliographic searching; it is one among many such tools. Library catalogues have not been designed to provide *the* bibliography on a topic as a list of items retrieved.[23] They have been designed to provide *a* bibliography, a start-

---

[21] For example, compare the 142,000,000 matches for the search *database + quality* in Google (14 Sept. 2006) with the bibliography of the works consulted for this paper (for which, see below).

[22] The goals of the scholar's bibliography are rooted in the scholar's discipline and "a discourse unifying minds in a community through a method according to which they understand one another." (Svagelski-Liassine, 1990, p.833). It is this common language, asserting that some things are true and valuable while some are not, that makes debate, and therefore science, possible. Chazal (2003, p.132) observed that "If the Internet makes all researchers engender their own hierarchies, define their own priorities, manage their exclusions, we will no longer be constrained to learn the ways of the past but to create, each one of us, our own means of access and follow our own paths." Babb (2006) compared the researcher's bibliography (i.e. a bibliography created by scholars) with what she calls "auto-bibliography", the bibliography that results from a set of subject searches in a database or library catalog. She concludes: "As auto-bibliography supports bibliography, so may bibliography in turn support auto-bibliography. ... [T]hey are ultimately complementary resources, each orbiting and supporting the other." (p. 479-480).

[23] In the text of his article Graham (1990) selectively quotes and completely distorts the meaning of Altick's (1975) remark "a library catalogue is not a tool of scholarly bibliography" (p. 217). Fortunately he gives an expanded quote in a footnote where we read: "Except in a very few great libraries, which contain virtually everything printed on a topic, and for special limited problems, a library card catalogue is not a tool of scholarly bibliography. Since it is only a location-directory to a particular and limited stock of books... it should never be resorted to for the guidance that thorough research requires." (p. 218). Altick is writing about "the guidance that thorough

ing point with readily available material which will hopefully provide directions for further inquiry. The chief difference between the library catalogue and Google is that the material described in a library catalogue is a deliberately limited set of materials which have been selected by subject specialists to be included in the library because of their value for research and (hopefully) described by persons sharing the intellectual commitments and scholarly vocabulary of the authors of those materials. None of this can be said of the items retrieved via a Google search. The Google search permits no filter (other than the hidden algorithms!) between the information and the user, and hence 426,000 responses to a query.[24]

Filtering, choosing and promoting certain materials over others in order to serve the institution's purposes are among the chief tasks of the library according to Wojciechowski (2004). The library itself as an organization is a deliberate attempt to restrict the universe of information to those fitting a particular purpose, whether the broad research goals of a large research library or the narrow goals of a nuclear reactor control room library. Evaluation and selection precede incorporation of materials into the library. The catalogue represents yet a further restriction in its attempt to describe each item with the library's users in mind. Libraries do not attempt to organize all the world's information for every conceivable purpose and every possible user and that is why libraries work in ways that a universal system such as Google does not and cannot work. In short, academic library catalogues represent the creation of information about a collection developed specifically for research purposes whereas Google represents mechani-

---

research requires" and that, as any researcher knows, requires a lot of time working in specialized bibliographies and periodical and conference paper indexes, bibliographies and indexes that the library catalogue will help you find but the indexing of which will not be included in the library catalogue itself. Altick did *not* advise his readers not to use the library catalogue, but only not to assume that it is a one-stop, one-size-fits-all information depot. The same arguments apply to the ill-informed view of Google as librarians imagine it and as Google advertises today: Google is also not a one-stop, one-size-fits-all information depot. Like Google, the library catalogue *is* a tool of research because it directs you to those more detailed sources of bibliographical information, no matter what size the library.

[24] Cf. Jochum and Wagner (1998, p.19): "What is concealed behind the output, no one can know."

cal matching of meaningless alpha-numeric sequences in an information universe with more useless than useful information.

In the information world of the Internet, making sense of the world's information requires not the creation of still more misinformation and nonsense but discarding a great deal of the "information" that is available.

> With the massive amount of information available nowadays thanks to the networking of the planet and in particular via the web, there are endless discussions on the virtues, properties and techniques of data mining. The problem today is not so much accessing information, but to identify good-quality information, then information relevant to the matter under consideration, and finally information exactly on target. (Heck, 2001, p.11)

More than 70 years ago Fabietti declared that "the essential matter is that the library not be a mere dispenser of books, a mechanical distributor of printed matter, but above all an enlightened guide for the reader." (Fabietti, 1933, p.15; quoted in Galli, 2001, p. 240).[25] Harvey (2002) suggested that the task of the library and the librarian today is no longer the diffusion of information—people do that themselves—but making sense of the information chaos readily available. Making sense implies the creation of meaning, and it is those meanings that libraries should be making available.[26]

III. Databases as Objects of Policy

The importance of the social insertion and integration of technologies in particular contexts was stressed by Capurro in his 1990 essay on "information ecology":

> Our field is full of futurological ideas, some of them 'planning' the next millennium. We can pollute ourselves with all kinds of utopias, which lead us nowhere, or, more precisely, to abandon the responsibility for evaluating risks and chances, of co-ordinating different possibilities for designing our knowledge universe and its channels, taking into account their specific quality. ... It is time, I think, to abandon the mode of technological 'grandiloquence' and to look for

---

[25] N.b.: he did not argue, he simply declared this to be the case, since this is a judgement about what libraries ought to be.
[26] For further discussion of sense making in libraries from a linguistic point of view, see Bade (2007a).

> more 'humble', i.e. more specific ways of establishing the limits of this expanding technology, and to act responsibly, conforming to the possibilities these limits offer! To see limits not as something negative but as the condition for plurality and interaction is a key point for the future of a technological society, i.e. for the insertion of technology within the complex of other 'traditions'. ... Information technology is not necessarily a pollution instrument nor is it an ideal artificial limb. We can profit from its own (!) potentialities if we are able to integrate it within the complexity of human communication. ... The information technology opens its potentialities if and only if we are able to interrelate it with the whole of its social dimensions. (Capurro, 1990, p.128-129)

In the literature of librarianship and information science databases, unlike library catalogues, are most often described as technical objects existing independently of their creators and users. The importance of policies for design, creation, implementation, maintenance and use are left out of consideration leading to the impossibility of understanding how databases actually (dis)function on site and in action. Examining databases and catalogues from the perspective of joint cognitive systems we can see that databases-in-use involve diverse groups of people involved in various tasks using a wide ranging system of tools, all of which are constructed and coordinated by policies.

Tasks, Tools and the Logic of Failure

When a task is successfully accomplished, the tool (technical system) is frequently assumed to provide the guarantee of that success while failure of the system is attributed to human error from 20% to 90% of the time (depending upon which rigorous scientific study you read).[27] Recent research on unsatisfactory outcomes (whether referred to as lack of quality, errors, failures, accidents, disasters or catastrophes) has led to a change in thinking and language, Hollnagel and Woods (2005) arguing that in the human information processing model of complex human-machine systems

> The separation between humans and machines achieved the status of a real problem ... and it became almost impossible to see it for what it really was—an artifact of the psychological application of the Shannon-Weaver model. (p. 17)

---

[27] Hollnagel (1993) provides a quick survey on p. 3 and tables on p.4-5.

What Hollnagel and Woods may not have realized was that the Shannon-Weaver model of communication (which they refer to as the "mother of all models") was lifted lock, stock and barrel from linguistics: Saussure's speech circuit as described and diagrammed in the *Cours de linguistique générale* (1916). It is fascinating to note that in the structural model of language described by Saussure there can be no misunderstanding and no errors since these are all expelled from linguistics proper (and hence from language).[28] For Saussure the system of language worked with mathematical exactitude; like many engineers and designers, Saussure believed that the system (*la langue*) could be studied abstracted from all contexts, human speakers, human intentions and communication situations. A translator of Saussure's *Cours* remarked recently that "only as long as we refrain from inquiring too closely into what might go wrong with it" can we continue to believe that it is the system that makes communication possible, and his remark could apply equally to models of information retrieval.[29]

Research in complex technical systems has noted that system designers must assume a certain implementation and use (spacio-temporal contexts, event situations, agents, organizational structures) while the actual use of those systems can be and often is very different from that imagined by the designer. If the designer's idea of the system—upon which all understanding and interpretation of the system is based—is rendered irrelevant by unexpected policies, structures or events, then when the systems are implemented, the results are often far from satisfactory. From the study of failure in socio-technical systems ergonomists have learned not only the limits of engineering design but also of the omnipresence of human agents in all technical systems, indeed their necessity, from designers to managers to law makers to line operators and maintenance workers. Human agents are in fact the chief source of dependability and reliability in technical systems (Poyet, 1990). Another lesson learned is how improvements

---

[28] Hollnagel and Woods (2005) reject the structural model of human-machine systems and insist upon a functional, situation and task oriented description, a theoretical critique with motivations and consequences similar to those developed by Roy Harris in linguistics (Harris (1973) and subsequent publications).

[29] Harris (2003), p.78. The passage quoted refers not to Saussure but to Wittgenstein's example of a hypothetical language of a builder and his assistant, a language limited to 4 words.

promised by technologies invariably lead to increased system complexity and hence to greater risks of system failure.

> Some of the explicit motivations for putting technology to use are reduced production costs, improved product quality, greater flexibility of services, and faster production and maintenance. It need hardly be pointed out that these benefits are far from certain and that a benefit in one area often is matched by new and unexpected problems in another. Furthermore, once the technology potential is put to use this generally leads to increased system complexity. Although this rarely is the intended outcome, it is a seemingly inescapable side effect of improved efficiency or versatility. The increased system complexity invariably leads to increased task complexity, among other things (e.g., Perrow, 1984). ... The growing task complexity generally comes about because adding functionality to a system means that there is an overall increase in complexity, even if there are isolated improvements. (Hollnagel and Woods, 2005, p.4)

Research on quality often focuses on errors, but most publications in the area of database quality cite this as only one factor—as indeed it is, given most understandings of error. Evaluation of database quality has been largely a study of technical capabilities of systems rather than a study of the quality of the data or information itself. The etiology and social history of database errors has been perhaps the least studied aspect of database quality and the available research on the topic has been largely confined to quantitative studies and advice literature (what to do about errors) for systems administrators and database managers. Much of this is sensible but rarely is there much awareness of the systemic nature of the problem (design, construction, management, etc.). The accountant Clark (1990) makes two vital points but the language used reveals the limitations of his concern: data entry.

> You need to catch errors before they get into your system. ... [A]ttaining a high degree of accuracy may be expensive and you must consider various degrees of accuracy. You cannot tolerate any inaccuracy in computing a pay check but you can use estimates or less precise figures to illustrate a gross change or a shift in direction. (p. 35)

Certainly some errors matter and some do not, and how and why they enter a database are some of the most important questions to be asked. It would be a fine thing if previous studies of database error had paid more attention to these crucial matters rather than with merely counting misplaced p's and q's, periods and commas. Yet the real problem for the scientist, accountant and language teacher as for the librarian is to determine not only what errors matter, when and why, but what are the conditions which give rise to these errors. Fujita and Hollnagel (2004) point out that "second-generation HRA [human reliability analysis] approaches ... emphasise that the likelihood of something being done incorrectly is determined by the performance conditions rather than by inherent human error probabilities" (p. 145).

In the 1980's American researchers led by Karl Weick studied high reliability organizations (HRO's) revealing that there were organizations in which accidents were so rare as to appear nonexistent, a fact that much earlier research had not noticed and theory had declared impossible (e.g. Perrow, 1984). In Sweden and Germany cognitive psychologists led by Berndt Brehmer and Dietrich Dörner put human managers in control of computer simulated human ecologies and studied the decisions and self-reports of the thinking and decision making of the participants. The reasoning of the managers seemed rational and was always well-intentioned but the results of these simulations were largely catastrophic failures. The inadequacies of human thought in the context of complex systems Dörner labeled "the logic of failure." Exactly as in the case of research on high reliability organizations, a clear formulation of the organization's goals in concrete terms and attitudes towards errors and error correction largely determined the success of the projects.

> We have become acquainted with many inadequacies of human thought in dealing with complex systems. We have seen people fail to formulate their goals in concrete terms, to recognize when their goals contradict one another, and to set clear priorities. We have also seen them badly mishandle temporal developments. Above all, we have seen people fail to correct their errors. (Dörner, 1997, p.185)

One finding has been that vague or general goals hide a multiplicity of goals under a single label. Dörner's comments on unclear goals include as one example "We have to make the library more user-friendly," a goal that lacks any "criteria by which we can decide with certainty whether the goal has been achieved." (Dörner, 1997, p.50-

51) It is a lofty and noble goal but at the same time as a guide for practical action it is a meaningless one.

> The goal we set... was to provide for the "well-being of the citizens." This goal is of no use whatsoever as a guidepost for action. Why? Well, what does "well-being" mean? Quite a lot and quite a few different things and, therefore, without further definition, nothing at all. (Dörner, 1997, p.58)

Different goals, implicit in the general goal but not explicitly recognized, may be linked directly, inversely or may contradict one another. In the library literature this was stated with admirable clarity by Peter Graham in 1990: "Quality in cataloging is inversely proportional to cataloging productivity. ... For present purposes, let us consider quality as having two aspects: extent and accuracy. *Extent* refers to how much information is provided in the record; *accuracy* refers to the correctness of what is provided." (Graham, 1990, p.213-214) To make matters more interesting, he refers the reader to a cataloging recon project "in which only the aspect of extent was considered, not any issue of accuracy" (Graham, 1990, p. 217), providing some justification for Thomas' (1996) remarks on the shifting emphasis of cataloging managers towards quantitative considerations. In the matter of accuracy the purely technical capacities of the current generation of library databases and searching systems has led many librarians to adopt what Dörner called a "repair service policy," a managerial approach to errors responsible for numerous catastrophic developments in his experiments. Such policies are evident in libraries in the use of post-cataloging enhancement services to provide authority control (e.g. MARS) and completeness (e.g. Marcadia) through automatic batch processing rather than ensuring accuracy and completeness at the point of entry into the catalogue.

> Subjects fail, for instance, to get their goals clear and then act according to a "repair service policy." They do this by eliminating the obvious errors and solving the conspicuous problems, while disregarding the less conspicuous ones and, of course, failing to take into account aberrant developments that first become apparent in faint symptoms. Subjects fail to construct an adequate picture of a complex, interconnected system. Often enough they do not treat a system as if it were a system, but like an accumulation of disconnected variables that can be manipulated in isolation. In this way, the long term and side effects of their actions remain obscure to them. (Dörner, 1990, p. 467-468)

Dörner also acknowledged that money is of great importance: without funding, no projects move from ideas to realities. For librarians like Calhoun, Graham and Marcum, a cost-benefit analysis is an absolute necessity and the goals are timeliness and quantity, not accuracy or fullness of information. High reliability organizations, like every other organization, operate on a budget, but like scientists, scholars, artists, philosophers and lovers—and unlike library managers—they do not operate according to a cost-benefit analysis and put reliability before profit and all persons involved understand and share these goals.

How organizations regard errors and policies concerning quality control are aspects of the same problem. Weick, Sutcliffe and Obstfeld (1999) noted that preoccupation with failure was one of the most important and characteristic traits of high reliability organizations, and that "a chronic worry in HROs is that analytic error is embedded in ongoing activities" (p. 91). One manager of a notable and much studied highly reliable organization—Admiral Rickover of the US Navy—believed that when mistakes are not reported "those in charge become disconnected and disoriented" (Bierly and Spender, 1995, p. 651). Yet it is not just error reporting, quality control policies and clear goals that determine the success or failure of an organization to meet its goals. The structure of organizations and an organization's links to other organizations may also be important factors in success and failure.

Morel (2003) noted that the division of labour was a primary factor in the making and perpetuation of what he called "absurd decisions," decisions radically and persistently in opposition to the desired goals. Weick, Stucliffe and Obstfeld (1999) echoed Perrow's concerns when they pointed to the growing problems related to comprehension of complex systems of networks and global interconnectedness:

> Turner's data show that it is commonplace for disasters to happen "when a large complex problem, the limits of which were difficult to specify, was being dealt with by a number of groups and individuals usually operating in separate organizations." This suggests that reliability will be an emerging concern as organizations increasingly participate in interorganizational networks because interorganizational coordination is so difficult to achieve and because the system becomes more complex and harder to comprehend. (p. 112)

Hollnagel (1993) defined a highly reliable system as "one that performs according to the requirements of the task across a range of different initial conditions and different working conditions. This is quite important because we do not always know in detail all the conditions under which the system may be called upon to function." (p. 79) If we accept such a definition, the quality of the research library catalogue should therefore be evaluated on the basis of how well it enables the researcher to utilize the particular collection indexed by the catalogue, whether that user is the expert, the librarian, the novice or the dilettante. How to evaluate that is another question.

It should not be difficult for the reader to see the significance of these lessons from ergonomics for librarianship. How do institutional policies determine the quality of the institution's databases? Since quality depends upon goals, the setting of goals and the means of satisfying those goals as matters of policy have a crucial importance in the end result. Failure to obtain the desired results is often, however, identified as the result not of policies but of the mistakes, errors or insufficiencies of some hapless person near the end of the work flow—a data entry person, a (copy-)cataloger—or else the technologies in use.[30] These latter are in fact the conclusions not only of library management but of the literature on database/catalogue quality as well. In contrast, the ergonomic literature of the past 30 years has increasingly focused attention on policies as producing the conditions that generate failure and one prime condition for failure is the existence of conflicting goals enshrined in policies.

University Librarian of Cornell University Library and former head of cataloging at the Library of Congress Sarah Thomas (1996) noted that cataloging managers' definitions of quality had shifted from concerns about quality to concerns about quantity: the quality of the information retrieved in a database search matters less than the quan-

---

[30] Duclos (1989, p. 127) remarked that attention "is systematically turned toward the operator rather than to accept any criticism of conceptions or modes of organization." Rickover (1979, p.16) commented that policies are often the biggest mistake but managers "blame those beneath them or those who preceded them" rather than their own policies. Locating failure at the end of the process prevents the manager from understanding the consequences of policies and ultimately leaves the manager disconnected and disoriented, fundamentally out of touch with the actual state of the organization.

tity of items retrieved.[31] Regarding quantity as the sole measure of quality—bigger is better—and disregarding all other factors in the performance of tasks and the evaluation of tools follows what has been described as the "logic of failure." Her article is in fact a remarkable document in which almost every policy described and praised exhibits the most common etiologies of failure identified in the literature on human error, ergonomics, high reliability organizations, joint cognitive systems and reliability engineering. Those cataloging management policies are: minimal level cataloging, outsourcing, turning attention away from errors in the interest of increased production, copy-cataloging without review, and cost rather than research value as the determining factor in production.

Conflicting Goals and Library Policies

> Multiple, simultaneously active goals are the rule, rather than the exception, for virtually all domains in which expertise is involved. Practitioners must cope with the presence of multiple goals, shifting between them, weighing them, choosing to pursue some rather than others, abandoning one, embracing another. Many of the goals encountered in practice are implicit and unstated. In specific situations, goals often conflict; ... Any adequate analysis of a field of practice requires explicit description of the interacting goals, how they contribute to tradeoffs and dilemmas in particular situations, and how practitioners can handle them. (Woods and Hollnagel, 2006, p.152)

Whereas Graham (1990) presented the conflict between productivity and quality in inverse fashion (organizations can have more of one only at the expense of the other), Ørsted (2001) questioned this opposition on what I regard as the most appropriate grounds: the client

---

[31] Chyan Yang, Keng-Chieh Yang and Hsu-Chieh Yuan (2007) of the National Chiao Tung University Institute of Information Management have recently made the opposite claim: "The quality of search results has indeed become more important than the quantity of search results." (p. 234), basing their claim on studies of searching strategies: "In the study, 50 percent of participants looked at only the top seven listings of the search results, and only 20 percent of participants looked at all top ten of the search results ... The way people search implies that the precision rate is more important than the recall rate." (p. 236). The "quantitative" shift that is apparent among library administrators is not apparent outside the insular world of library managers and technology salesmen.

determines the level of quality desired, with all matters of cost and productivity following from that.Ganińska (2000) and others influenced by TQM literature adopt this perspective, leading to a radically different managerial orientation. From this perspective, there is no "inversely proportional" relationship between productivity and quality; rather there is simply a question of what the clients demand, and therefore the possible range of costs and productivity levels are also determined by the client's demands. No cost-benefit analysis is relevant, the client's demands are the determining factor. In the case of the library, how the library discovers and meets those demands are very different matters, and there the real problems lie. As Santarsiero (2001, p.79) lamented "Balancing the diverse demands is not easy, especially when they are contradictory." Do we serve the world via the Internet, or a particular group of users? Are we answerable to the faculty or to the bursar? (Certainly to both, but in very different fashion.) Do we supply detailed metadata for everything or for a judiciously selected subset of materials, everything else getting a different (e.g. less full, less costly) treatment? If so, how do we make that selection? If not, does that mean that everything collected in a library has an equal value, that nothing is more important than anything else? When and how is timeliness a factor? Are librarians users or should their uses be ignored in discussing the library's needs? A brief look at some of the conflicting goals that libraries have to consider follows.

Knowledge organization vs Information supply

Do libraries supply predigested information or do they create bibliographical information to support original research? Surely the answer must be that they do both. Any library which intends to support research must have an information system (and by system I mean not only the technical tools, but the intellectual content, personnel and organizational support which those tools require for their successful operation) that can perform what Thomas Mann calls the "heavy-lifting capacity" of a research library. In order to understand the level of bibliographic control which serious research requires it is not enough to look at information practices in a single field (e.g. computer science), since the needs of the various disciplines now, if not always, differ widely in terms both of languages of publication, historical depth and even the necessity of knowing the literature. It is unfortunate that much of the LIS discussion of information needs of "scientists" has accepted as its typical case information science, in which one can indeed limit one's reading to the last five years' online publications in English and still produce a paper that will be published. This is not the case for much research carried out in the humanities and social sciences. A narrow and impoverished understanding of the great diversity of needs and styles of research has led to no distinction being made between the needs and current practices of a high-school student writing a five page paper and those of a Hungarian lexicographer, an archeologist in Yunnan or an ecologist studying the reptilian fauna of the Okawango Delta. The kind of information system which will satisfy both the high-school student and the senior researcher will require a great deal of information creation and organization, whether the high-school student appreciates or uses it at all.

Yet why should the goals of information creation and knowledge organization conflict with those of information provision? The answer may be found in how these are understood in the planning and provision of services. The support of research at the graduate level and beyond requires an enormous investment in materials and a bibliographic searching system capable of guiding the researcher through not only the locally available literature but also that which may be obtained from external sources. Collection development and indexing and abstracting tools (printed or electronic, catalogue or database) are all costly and labor intensive. If in order to save money library planners attempt to serve serious research with a searching system designed merely for information provision (essentially turning the library into an Answers.com), failure is guaranteed for the researcher. An information system designed to provide ready made Facts-on-File or static answers to questions cannot satisfy a researcher intent on investigating the origins, assumptions, reasons and contexts of these facts and answers, much less one intent on proving them wrong.

Completeness vs Timeliness

The chief problem with missing data was stated succinctly by an employee of the world's largest bibliographic database—Glenn Patton of OCLC—in an email to the author concerning the lack of vernacular script data in OCLC: "The basic issue is that we cannot index data that is not there." (Thank you, Glenn.) One common reason why that data is not in the record is that such data has to be created and someone must pay for that. Marc Truitt's recent remark on Autocat contains an elegant formulation of the deeper reason why most attempts to solve the dilemma of backlogs and budget cuts by eliminating information creation have not been well received by many involved in the latter activity:

> Attempting to trivialize this or that element or rule does not move us forward in addressing the larger contradiction between our growing thirst for reliable and complete bibliographic metadata and the fact that we exist in a climate where we are increasingly unable or unwilling to pay for that metadata. (Marc Truitt, posting to AUTO-CAT, 30 August 2006)

And a serious contradiction it is. Were that contradiction recognized by library administrators, efforts would be directed towards documenting the desire, need and value of increasing information creation rather than justifying the abandonment of that activity.[32]

In the 1950's and 1960's there was great excitement in the library world as information scientists began to design and put into operation information systems which finally promised a technical solution to the quantitative and qualitative problems of information handling and control. In the 1970's and 1980's users like myself became aware of the gross inadequacy of so much of the information which had been entered into those early systems, often because the nature of those systems and their limitations were not clearly understood or foreseen.[33]

---

[32] What, for instance, does it mean that American library administrators are constantly presenting economic arguments in favor of reducing the information content of bibliographic records while Cuban librarians are presenting forceful economic arguments for the importance of libraries adding value through analysis of documents? "Rapid and efficient access to precise and reliable information permits one to take an adequate stance when decisions for solving problems at the least cost must be made. This is only possible if there has been a previous analysis of the information with the values of the intended users of the information in mind and that information added." (Valdés Abreu, 2001, p. 2)

[33] Cf. Abbott (2006): "In summary, the main lesson that comes from a reflection about technology is that library researchers have to become much more aware of what technologies actually can and cannot do, much more aware of what is actually going on underneath the metacrawlers and ostensible union catalogues, much more involved in training students to see behind the technological front. ... But the future of serious library scholarship lies in a criti-

For example, abbreviations of great importance in permitting the totality of information available to be written onto a small card were simply uninterpretable by the electronic systems, and therefore never included in the search results of these latter. Information implicit in the original script, format and punctuation was lost in this same technical translation. A system of metadata appropriate for printed cards failed when mechanically transferred to electronic form, whereas much valuable material on the cards was lost due to the technical limitations of the electronic systems.

Yet no sooner had these serious failures of the previous generation become painfully evident to library users than librarians began advocating minimal records in an electronic environment where for the first time all of the information input could be utilized. This movement continued apace in the 1990's with the adoption of Core Level records and then into the 21st century as Cornell University libraries, booksellers and others began flooding shared databases with below minimal records. At present (Summer 2006), the technical capacities for information retrieval are vast but the policies in place throughout the United States all prevent the utilization of those capacities because they almost all involve the non-provision of information, i.e. the repudiation of the goal of access to information.[34] Oddy (1999) declared "Change should not be resisted solely because it means we will do things differently from the way we have done them before, but it should and must be resisted if it lessens or inhibits access to the content of the collection" (p. 38), and then offered one of the most balanced discussions of less than full cataloging that I have read:

> Is it better to have fuller records, but fewer of them, or to have briefer records and fuller coverage of the collection? Both diminish access—but the former diminishes access to the collection as a whole, whilst extending it, possibly, to those bibliographic items fortunate enough to be catalogued. On the understanding that a briefer record is still a standard record, containing core, critical data for retrieval, when a choice has to be made then I would always opt

---

cally constructive and intense engagement with technology, not a running from it or a welcoming embrace."

[34] One of the most recent of these policies is the much touted Access Level for description. Giving the name of Access to a record designed specifically to eliminate information in the bibliographical record is certainly worthy of Orwell's Newspeak, is it not?

for extended coverage over in-depth cataloguing. Again I need to emphasise, though, that such decisions must take place within the context of a clear strategy. You don't just cut the record in response to a cut in the budget. (p. 38-39)

I have only one objection: some materials are worth more than others; this has always been the case and always will be. Yet what is important for any given library will be determined by the purposes which the library serves, and a cooperative or shared database requires that local differences of purpose and emphasis be addressed through local attention and adaption of every record not locally created.[35]

Few minimalists, however, have any strategy other than doing less and calling it more, faster, cheaper and even better. Instead of accepting the challenge to study the impacts of leaner records and arguing for the value of information creation, most advocates of less-than-full cataloging accept the financial situation and seek to cut services, all the while claiming that nothing is lost.[36] The claim that these records will meet user needs is based not on changing user needs but on the denial of their existence. Fortunately, some librarians recognize that the increased searching capacity of current technologies have led to an increase rather than a decrease in user demands: "users demand access to ever more detailed bibliographic information, including tables of contents, keywords, summaries, etc." Bereijo (1999) observed, and indeed the library world is schizophrenic on this issue.

The arguments for all of these practices have been the same: doing something takes more time than not doing something; therefore, let us not do something so that we can save time (and money), timeliness being the sole criteria of quality.[37] What is diminished in every case is

---

[35] On the problem of different strokes for different folks, see the papers in Freon (1996), especially Thibault and Freon (1996) and Maisonneuve (1996).
[36] For one example, read the opening sentence of *Access Level Record for Serials Working Group Final Report July 24, 2006*: "Declining library budgets, competition from Internet search engines and information services, and the escalating costs of cataloging have caused libraries to emphasize ways to meet user needs while decreasing costs." The remainder of the report is a magnificent example of junk science in the service of the agenda of one particular group of librarians. For a brief discussion, see Bade (2006b).
[37] Cf. Górny (2002): "measuring time is of course not the only method of evaluating the quality of library services."

access, and it is the user who suffers the increased cost in time and effort. Graham (1990) acknowledged and defended this transfer of costs, suggesting that the user should shoulder an increasing amount of the costs since libraries lack the necessary funds. Unfortunately, it is not so simple, for if the information is not created in the first place, neither the user nor the technology can create or manipulate missing information: without the necessary information the literature search does not merely become more costly for the user, but in fact it becomes impossible (and of course not in any sense timely). The belief that what now matters is not bibliographic description but the searching system has led to the current situation in which we have a First World information system crippled by Fourth World information lack.

Efficiency vs Quality
(Mercedes Benz vs. Moped vs. Tricycle)

Efficiency is not exactly the same as timeliness, nor ought quality to be understood as equivalent to completeness, yet these conflicts are often treated as nearly identical because they both mask the simple desire to save money. A vocal advocate of efficiency, Graham's (1990) opening salvo was quoted above: "Quality in cataloging is inversely proportional to cataloging productivity." (p. 213). What Graham and his many admirers fail to acknowledge is that striving for efficiency can and often does lead to results contrary to the organization's goals.

> The constant striving for improved efficiency often leads to multiple and sometimes inconsistent goals, organisational pressures, and clumsy technological solutions. The contemporary work environment can be characterised as follows:
>
> - Cognition is distributed rather than isolated in the mind of a thoughtful individual, and cooperation and coordination are ubiquitous. Operators are embedded in larger groups and organisations, which together define the conditions for work, the constraints and demands as well as resources.
>
> - People do not passively accept technological artefacts or their general conditions of their work but actively and continuously adapt their tools and activities to respond to irregularities and disturbances, and to meet new demands.

- Technological development is rampant, leading ... inevitably to greater operational complexity.

- Technology is often used in ways that are not well adapted to the needs of the operator. ... As the complexity of systems grow it manifests itself as an apparent epidemic of failures labelled 'human error'. (Hollnagel and Woods, 2005, p.37-38)

It has been widely noted that one of the crucial characteristics of organizations with a very low rate of failure is that they put reliability (quality, success, safety) first and do not rely upon cost-benefit analyses in the determination of policies and procedures. Any examination of the cost of information provision will clearly reveal the high cost of manual description, analysis and indexing. Were matters otherwise there would be little incentive to look for ways to improve efficiency, reduce costs, develop automated indexing systems, scanning technologies and so on. Unfortunately, if one wants good description and indexing as a basis for mechanical exploitation, optical scanning and automatic indexing are severely limited in the amount of information which they can provide, and even more limited in terms of the accuracy and usefulness of the information which they can supply.[38] Information technologies are, in fact, limited in almost exactly the same fashion as a human indexer lacking the capacity for reading and understanding, the principal difference being that these labours of incomprehension can be accomplished much quicker by machine.

It is also possible to improve efficiency and cut costs while retaining many catalogers simply by reducing the amount of interpretation involved (in the manner of Cornell's COR, for which see below), but this entails losing all of the information created by those acts of interpretation *and* an accounting system which does not indicate this loss on the negative side of the balance; to acknowledge the loss would negate any hoped for gains in efficiency (Sapori, 1995). Indeed, if efficiency is measured solely in terms of the time it takes to move physical items from mailroom to the shelf, then no interpretation or information creation of any sort is necessary: a barcode on the item and in the

---

[38] Cf. the sceptical remarks on automated classification in Oberhauser (2005) and Golub (2006), and Heck's remarks on automated methodologies (Heck, 2001, p.11): "Beware also of what is sometimes said on automated methodologies. Spontaneous generation of knowledge does not exist as no methodology will ever reveal knowledge that is not already somehow in the data."

computer will move books, computer files and periodicals along as quickly as homogenous blocks of stone bearing no information at all. At a more reasonable level of analysis, questions regarding authority control for names, series titles, and subjects and their possible replacement by keyword searching by tag or general searching over all elements in the record are decided on the basis of judgements concerning the necessity or value of information (metadata) creation for information systems: if one regards metadata as no longer necessary in today's (or tomorrow's) information systems, arguments from efficiency will undoubtedly conclude that metadata is unnecessary, whereas if one regards metadata as necessary now and perhaps also in future information systems, then efficient utilization of the information systems *presupposes* the creation of information. And that means people, since "the machine does not create facts (every element left out is definitely lost), nor does it create the contexts of the facts." (Beaudiquez, 1991, p.199).

In many matters monetary costs can be decreased through savings in labour and time but always at a high cost in information loss since it is simply not true that current technologies can do for the user what the human cataloger can. It is only when the capacities of information technologies are misunderstood and the serious researchers' needs ignored that one can believe the elimination of certain value adding tasks constitute an increase in efficiency.[39] It is interesting to compare the attitudes towards technologies (especially information technologies) in libraries with that found in economics (Eymard-Duvernay, 1989), translation services (Ørsted, 2001), accounting (Clark, 1990) and the ergonomics literature (Bainbridge, 1987; Parasuraman and Riley, 1997; Poyet, 1990; Vestrucci, 1990) where one finds a much more accurate appraisal of both the capacities and limitations of technologies, the necessity of human judgement, and the importance of accuracy and error management.

Eymard-Duvernay offered the following remarks on the relation between price and quality:

---

[39] Once again, Heck (2001, p.11) has stated the matter succinctly: "As a general rule, the quality of results can at best reflect the quality of the input material when dealing with data-related methodologies (in other words, garbage in can only lead to garbage out). With the tools we have today, increase of quality is still the result of time and human sweat."

> In the market model, a difference of quality is immediately translatable into terms of price... Such an equilibrium is broken if among the external constraints determining quality some are not translatable into market terms. This is the case for example whenever there is a question of security and human lives are at stake, or wherever the industrial constraints are unalterable. If the product is an element in a chain of industrial fabrication, the necessary coherence of the whole prohibits playing around with quality. Price fluctuations cannot compensate for the poor precision of a piece... A disproportion appears between the failure and the monetary consequences. Automobile subcontractors are always under such pressure from the manufacturers: the smallest defects can derail complete product lines. (1989, p.354-355)

Focusing on the risks associated with bibliographic database construction brings a different perspective to the discussion of quality: it is no longer simply a matter of personal preferences but the adequate functioning of that element considered to be the foundation of our present economy and society: information. Denis (2006) argued that one of the chief factors in the genesis of accidents and catastrophes is an ignorance or insufficient understanding of the risks involved.

Ørsted (2001) demonstrated a clear understanding of the importance of information technologies in the production of translations in a competitive market:

> The tools permit an increase in speed, but at the cost of quality if they are not used with care and adapted to the particular needs of the company in question. Customers have realised that there are no short cuts and miracles to be found in the use of translation technology, still the demand for speed is unrelenting as competition becomes fiercer. So the translator is caught between the claim for speed and the personal ambition of delivering the ultimate quality. Shall the two ever meet? (p. 440)

Unlike librarians who so often insist that 89.73% of library users will be satisfied with a flat tire and neither need nor want a John Deere, she recognizes that even the latest technologies cannot provide what the demanding patron requires: the human translator is still necessary.

> Although they have improved considerably over the past years and leverage the industry in delivering highly sophisticated service, they can still only be used as the tools they are to serve translators to make them more efficient. (Ørsted, 2001, p. 442)

Here we see a language completely opposed to the language of library management. Information technologies are only tools which require human intelligence and judgement to render them efficient. Instead of claiming on the one hand that the users do not need sophisticated systems or on the other that sophisticated systems require no human intelligence, she insists that technologies are important tools for translators to use in their efforts to supply more translations faster and cheaper, if not better. Her remarks on quality are also interesting: customers cannot produce the quality but they can judge it. And in her translation company, the level of quality demanded by the client determines the price, not vice-versa.[40]

Conflicting standards

Quality standards have been damned as leading to massive backlogs. It is true that in the absence of adequate staff to do the necessary work, producing high quality work will always lead to backlogs, no matter what the context. However, rather than documenting, stressing the importance of and arguing for adequate staffing, library administrators pride themselves on lowering standards. Nevertheless, library administrators do have a valid point: one need only look at the useless notes and the time it takes some catalogers to complete a record to admit that something is wrong with the standards as they are revealed in practice. Yet standards are not something to be dispensed with so easily; they have very strong arguments in their favour. Aracil (1982) argued that the primary purpose of standard forms was to facilitate communication across times and spaces. In technological systems,

---

[40] On the relation of price to quality there is an extensive economics literature, briefly summarized in Debril (2005) who writes: "In effect, if the buyers are incapable of distinguishing good from bad quality, all merchandise can be sold at the same price, which both discourages the introduction of new products in the market and encourages the sale of mediocre products. If the quality depends on the price and not the contrary, "bad quality drives out good", and the market ceases to exist (Akerlof, 1970)." (p. 206) Librarians are betting rather heavily that library users will be unable to distinguish between the value of a library catalog producing 2 matches in response to a search for "Mongol + Java" and Google's 430,000+ useless matches for the same search—or at least that our users will not care. Do library administrators really understand the market and the importance of quality in its workings?

standards are imperative, and even moreso for shared or networked systems.

> Nowadays it is unthinkable to not distinguish the titles, patronyms or identical names of corporate bodies. The identical titles of periodicals are often differentiated by the aid of the name of the town, date of publication, of the issuing body or periodicity; the homonymous authors by dates or specialities... (Witt, 1993, p.39).

The use of standards requires training not only of the librarians who implement them but of the users who need to adequately understand what the standards prescribe in order to fully utilize the system, which is to say that standards are costly for both librarians and other library users. For this reason, and perhaps for this reason alone, many librarians have advocated a variety of new standards—Core Level, Access Level—as well as advocating the use of minimal and even below minimal level "standards." In all of these various standards, the goal is to reduce human involvement (time and attention) in the creation of bibliographical information, thereby reducing costs to the library. In every case the manner in which human involvement is reduced is to eliminate (i.e. declare unnecessary) certain types of information (e.g. notes), forms of information (e.g. precoordinated subject strings), and certain quality control measures (e.g. the use and creation of established headings). In short, by having standards which permit the non-creation of information the goal of reduced human-related costs is met, but goals related to the needs of both technical systems and users are not.

Access or Not?

> A catalogue has minimum requirements below which it cannot be called a catalogue. The problem is the definition of those requirements. (Guerrini, 2002, p.21)

It is not difficult to see that in the above conflicts of goals there is little more than a proliferation of terms to mask a single conflict of interests: the creation of information, for whatever purpose, takes time, intelligence and money; the less information that is created, the less the costs will be *to the library* (the actual costs are simply transfered to the user). The problem for the administrator as for the cataloger is to determine what information is important and what can be left undone. Any task which can be left undone will result in more, cheaper and faster; any task which cannot be left undone but is nevertheless not done will not lead to more, cheaper and faster: it will only result in a failure to satisfy the primary goals which alone justify the existence of the institution. Some current policies productive of bibliographic failure will be the topic of the next section.

Policies that Court Failure

There are innumerable policies that can negatively impact catalogue quality. I mention here only a select few connected with various areas of responsibility: classification methodology, cataloging standards, outsourcing (vendors, copy-cataloging, etc.), and distribution of work responsibilities.

Classification assignment

Classification systems for libraries were designed for the express purpose of shelving library materials by design rather than simply by order of their arrival. Classification systems allow for the shelf order to impart information about the contents of the items on the shelf, much as the order of elements on a traditional catalogue card imparted information beyond the information explicitly recorded. The assignment of classification numbers is therefore not merely a position indicator for finding a particular item, but also a subject searching system. In a library using such a classified system for the spatial ordering of material the classification number is therefore a crucial component of the information system considered in its totality.[41] The assignment of classification numbers therefore requires an analysis of the subject of the material; to assign such a classification number without basing it upon that analysis would render the system itself of no use, a waste of effort, time and money. Yet it is just this that some libraries now do. The evidence of this may be found in their catalogues and policy statements.

One policy instituted at the Joseph Regenstein Library in the mid 1990's was designed specifically to remove the work of classification from the professional staff and make it the responsibility of clerks who would of course be paid much less than the professionals. Yet in order to justify giving this task to non- (para-) professionals it was necessary

---

[41] Cf. the remarks of Abbott (2006) quoted above.

to argue that it could be done mechanically, that it is a task requiring neither learning nor intelligence. The argument presented was that since the call number should match the first subject heading, any record found in the shared database which lacked a class number but had a subject heading would be given to the non-professional staff who could then simply search the local catalogue for that subject heading and give the same class number to the item in hand. What that heading was, whether it was correct, inadequate, irrelevant or in a foreign language did not matter, although there were of course more detailed instructions about what to do if the heading in the record did not exist in the local catalogue, if it were in another language, etc. For the purposes of this section, the details do not matter: what matters are the assumptions that the subject heading did not need to be evaluated and that an appropriate class number for the item in hand could simply be taken from other items with that same subject heading.

The first matter of significance is simply that the task has been changed from one of understanding and interpreting to a mindless task of matching. It has become a task ripe for automation; even if the "machines" performing the task are biologically speaking human, the work they do is precisely the kind of task for which machines are desireable and available. The second matter of significance is that judgement is no longer involved, eliminating any possibility for intelligent intervention (unless, of course, the thinking clerk wants to suffer the wrath of a supervisor). Thirdly, the catalogue is locked into a never-ending cycle of repeating past interpretations, even when these were mistaken in the first place: error correction becomes impossible because both interpretation and judgement have been eradicated from the process. Consequently, the classification system itself will become an absurdity and the entire process a mockery of knowledge organization.

In Bade (2004) I discussed what I believe to be one example of this policy, and discovered upon further investigation a related classification disaster. A record found in OCLC had a class number for the US Army War College in Carlisle, PA, when it was in fact about the role of NATO and Russia in matters of national security in Eastern Europe. I searched the contributing library's catalogue and found to my amazement that there were scores of books listed under this class number, only a handfull of them having as their subject that College. In large part, the items under this class number—no matter what the subject—were published by the College, leading me to suspect that far from reflecting LC practice (as indicated by the metadata in the bibliographical record) these class assignments were based on publisher, not subject. The particular book which had led me on this search was not published by the College, but had a subject heading (albeit an inappropriate one) which matched headings found in some of the other records. The result of these combined policies at Cornell can be examined by anyone who takes the time to browse UA413.A66 in the Olin Library Catalogue.

It is bad enough that these classification policies lead to absurd library catalogues; that the workers are reduced to mechanical units in a bureaucratic mockery of a scholarly institution and prohibited from exercising their intelligence and judgement is appalling.[42]

Do not think and do no research

It is not only non-professional staff who are prohibited from thinking and doing research: many of the rules and procedures for cataloging insist that the form to be entered into the record should be based solely on what is found on the piece in hand (even if that is insufficient or leads to conflicts or ambiguities in the database), prohibit the entering of information found on another item (e.g. another issue of a serial), use the form on the title page, even when very important additional information may be found elsewhere on the piece, etc. Certainly no one would desire rules that required external verification and justification of every element of the description, since often these are not to be found anywhere else than on the piece in hand; yet some of the rules as they exist (particularly for serials) frequently lead to the prohibition of including certain information or its later deletion by an "enhancing" library basing their description on a different volume, source of information or slightly different copy (i.e. defective copy, partial set).

One example discussed on Autocat provoked an interesting response from a cataloger at the Library of Congress. The issue involved creating an authority heading for the Hungarian Section of the BBC World Service. IF the cataloger were to fashion the heading according to the form found on the piece—following the rules (AACR2/LCRI)—the heading would be unlike all similar headings

---

[42] This reduction of humans from actors to spectators in organizations was the subject of a fascinating dissertation by Sotto (1990), *Man without knowledge*.

for sections of the BBC in our shared authority files. Following LC and UK's (consistent) usage would produce a form different from all those headings created by other (non-LC, UK) libraries, while following the forms created by other libraries would be inconsistent with LC/UK usage. Aaron Kuperman of LC responded with the following note:

> None of those are subject headings governed by LCSH (based primarily on reference sources). Rather they are names headings governed by AACR2/LCRI (based primarily on the name as it appears in the work being cataloged). The last time I advocated greater reliance on reference sources, in the interest of serving users, I was threated with serious sanctions by management, so I won't discuss the matter further. ... This note is NOT an official communication from the Library of Congress. (Kuperman, 2006)

A later Autocat discussion of similar matters took place during the month of August 2007. Helen Buehler remarked on the international dimension of this policy of non-research

> And it can also happen that a name is unique in one country, and another person in another country has the same name. Both would presumably be undifferentiated in their national NAFs—but what if a library in country 1 acquires a book (and authority record) by/for the person from country 2? If both had had dates on to start with, life would be much simpler for the cataloguer faced with the problem of who wrote which, or are they the same or... (Autocat, 31 August 2007)

and Gordon Pew very perceptively added:

> Cataloguing is an international activity these days. The notions of not qualifying a name with dates and other data unless a conflict arises with a similar name, the notion that one doesn't routinely add death dates to existing headings, the very fact of abiding undifferentiated names at all -- all work fine if you and I and the other person in the department know what we're looking at. It's as if the shoebox I keep under my bed containing information on, let's say, old American cars (I don't, really) were somehow found out about by everybody on the Internet. They would no doubt have all kinds of questions on why I did or didn't follow certain practices, why I ignored some crucial facts, and why I belabored everybody else with unimportant details. But I'd protest, I never expected Janet from Tulsa to see this stuff at all! (Autocat, 31 August 2007)

The severe problems with these prohibitions on research and practices such as limiting the source for authorized headings to the particular item in hand can be seen in the context of related materials—translations, multiple versions, variations in the practices of publishers and authors, potential for conflicts between names and series titles, etc.—and perhaps even more clearly in the varieties and limitations of searching strategies in the current technological situation. For example, browsing for subordinate bodies of a particular institution (such as the BBC) could yield all of these entities in an alphabetical list, but the rules specify using the form found on the particular piece that you have in hand, and if this is in a form other than that found in another publication by the same body, the established form may not and often is not discovered, leading to the multiplicity of forms in the bibliographical and authority files and a lack of cross-references. Consistency as well as notes and references based on research is immensely helpful to all and can often be provided by a very quick look at a reference source.

While faithfulness of description must be based solely on the item described, consistency of established forms and relationships between headings can often only be acheived by consulting external sources. Leaving aside the considerable benefits to library users that this research would provide, the benefits to librarians alone would justify the extra labour involved, especially in the current working environment in which many (most?) libraries suffer from a severe lack of language and subject expertise.

"A bibliographic record"

Librarians who have explored the possibilities for changing the nature of the work performed in libraries using networked information systems have realized that there is great potential for upgrading and correcting databases through batch processing of records. The work of acquisitions, collection development, cataloging and catalogue maintenance have all been changed through incorporating services such as CatMe and Marcadia from metadata vendors, booksellers and shared databases. The library sends a batch of records to the service to be matched against another file and these needed services will be supplied insofar as they can be identified by information (or the absence of it) in the original record, in the library's profile and in the records in the file against which the original is to be matched. These technical possibilities have led many to assume that what the local library now needs is nothing more than "a bibliographic record" which can be linked by a number, whether that be an accession number, LC, ISBN, OCLC control number, or some other. Any additional information required (authors, series, vernacular script, subjects) will be acquired at a later date by sending the number to a supplier who will check for whatever improved versions may be available. In theory this works splendidly (see the very clearly articulated discussion in Robertson and Barton, 2005), but in practice it has proven disastrous (Erbolato-Ramsey and Grover, 1994; Bade, 2003), since "the context of the wider environment, [and] its relationship with other relevant workflows" (Robertson and Barton, 2005, p.9) has been poorly understood or ignored. Such "data mining" can indeed be used to find information, but cannot evaluate it, and when the sources mined consist primarily of misinformation and impoverished files every file must be evaluated individually. The social insertion of technologies always results in the technologies working in a context for which they were not planned, and therefore "what is technologically possible is not always realizable" (González, 1997, p.265).

First of all, as in many industrial accidents, the potential of the technical system is evaluated without any understanding of what are the prerequisites for its successful implementation. In the case of information systems, the primary requirement is the availability of accurate and adequate information, something which cannot be guarranteed for any autonomous information source (Naumann, 2001). Secondly, the system is seen from the narrow perspective of what an individual library expects to get out of it, i.e. not as a system subject to all the inputs of participating institutions. If all libraries input the barest minimum of information into the system and wait for someone else to do the work, then there will never be any information beyond the initial minimal record.[43] Thirdly, whenever the work is performed mechanically, there can be no detection, identification or correction of errors other than those which are strictly determined by technical re-

---

[43] "In this study, the records from other RLIN members, which needed updating and were not later cataloged by LC, were never updated. This would seem to indicate that most libraries accept and input less than full AACR2 level records online and do not update them at a later time." (Erbolato-Ramsey and Grover, 1994, p. 83)

quirements or have been both proscribed and predicted (e.g. cross-references for subject terms in a thesaurus).[44]

Cataloging departments without requisite variety

The opposite of the immediately preceding approach ("a bibliographic record") can be found in libraries where certain materials are collected and cataloging is both desired and demanded by administration, but where there are no persons competent to provide that cataloging. This happens not only in work performed within libraries but also in materials cataloged by vendors of cataloging services (for examples and further discussion, see Bade, 2003 and 2004). This problem is compounded when this work is also performed according to the demands of quality programs such as **BIBCO**, **NACO** and **SACO**. In a study of bibliographic records bound for copy-cataloging Bade (2003) found that many PCC records clearly revealed that the cataloger(s) lacked the linguistic ability to interpret the title page much less the following text. Yet this did not prevent the catalogers from providing full cataloging, complete with multiple wrong subjects, corresponding classification and authority records.

As in so many problems in libraries, the pervasive lack of adequate personnel to accomplish the work which the materials acquired requires can be traced directly to pervasive beliefs about what technological advances will mean for library operations. The possibility of shared cataloging led to the beliefs that staff could be cut, not just in one library but everywhere. Yet while the number of items requiring original creation of bibliographical records certainly decreases with the possibility of shared cataloging, the range of linguistic skills and subject knowledge required in each institution does not decrease at all. In fact the opposite happens: the specialists have all disappeared and many if not most catalogers now have to catalog in all subjects (and formats), and many catalogers are responsible for materials in many languages which they do not know or know only cursorily. Material in "difficult" subjects and languages are either not catalogued, catalogued minimally, or catalogued incorrectly by persons ill-suited to the

---

[44] Even in the restricted context of a monolingual text such techniques as spell checkers can only indicate where there *might* be an input error, since the technology cannot know what is actually being transcribed from the item itself.

task. In a library with sufficient staff positions, the required knowledge and skills can be maintained in the library as a whole; with insufficient staff, that requisite variety cannot be maintained in the library because of the inherent limitations of human capacity for knowledge acquisition.

If the library cannot, for whatever reason, create bibliographic information that is accurate, then the library should not produce inaccurate information or otherwise pretend to offer the users services that in fact do not exist. Many libraries in areas outside the wealthy industrialized Euro-American sphere do not attempt detailed subject analysis but do offer a description which contains no misinformation. A good example may be found in the CIP data in many Romanian books: cataloging in publication supplied by the Romanian National Library is limited to the transcription of certain elements found on the title page, and a UDC class number. Subject headings and authorized headings are not offered. The result is a record that is accurate and useful for the limited purposes of identification and classification. In contrast to the limited information created by the Romanian library, when these same books are catalogued by US libraries into one of the shared utilities, the records are often incorrectly transcribed (e.g. wrong diacritics) and provided with subject headings and corresponding class numbers that have no relation to the subject of the book, i.e. they are not based on understanding and interpretation but merely on guesswork. (The fact that the number of ways in which one might describe a book for particular users and uses is unlimited does not mean that there are no incorrect descriptions.)

Although the policies discussed above are always put forth in the interest of the user ("more, faster, cheaper," etc.), whenever a library asks only for "a bibliographic record" or provides misinformation without any possible usefulness, the user has been eliminated from consideration in the construction of the information system. The library ceases to be an institution devoted to knowledge organization and information creation and becomes nothing more than a conveyor belt labeling bricks and brains in an identical fashion and moving them into the warehouse, as in the mathematical theory of communication.[45] As is so often the case, Dupuy has precisely identified the problems:

---

[45] In a fascinating article describing the move of artifacts from a museum to a new location Marty (2005) found that "By changing their focus from error

POLITICS AND POLICIES FOR DATABASE QUALITIES   63

> The theory of Shannon has two essential limitations...: it does not take into account the *meaning* of the information, nor does it take into account the *creation* of information. If one "forgets" this, then one can treat information as a thing..." (Dupuy, 1980, p.188)

As in Shannon and Weaver's model, librarianship is transformed into the management of conveyors and transportation systems, with no connection whatever with learning and scholarship, much less learners and scholars—the antithesis of the library envisioned by Di Domenico (2001).[46] An early reader of this paper (Barry Hinman of Stanford) described this sorry state of affairs, lamenting in his response to me "The bottom line really seems to be "throughput." Get it in, get it out: we are doing our job."

---

prevention to error recovery, museum staff members gained many benefits that went beyond their ability to detect and correct errors." (p. 318). This particular conclusion of the author cannot be transferred directly to the work of cataloging since all of the artifacts in this museum had all been described and labeled at a much earlier date by specialists and it was this thorough and accurate record in a database linked to the identification number on the items themselves which made it possible to treat all the museum's objects as nothing but objects with serial numbers. Had that description not been provided previously, the movers themselves would have had to have a knowledge adequate to recognize and identify all of the objects involved. The difference is similar to the book that arrives in a box in the library and that same book with a call number and catalogue record: the latter can be shelved with a high degree of reliability by anyone who knows only call number order; that same shelver confronted with the book as it first arrives in the library would have no idea where to shelve the volume (unless of course the shelf order was based on size, color or a purchase order number). Marty's other conclusions, however, are of considerable importance for library catalogue management and we shall return to some of them later.

[46] "Naturally, I am broaching the question—delicately, and only in passing—that all of this presupposes a library, and more generally an institutional environment in which sharing of knowledge is recognized as a value and in which each operator is guaranteed the necessary motivation for expressing himself independently and without any reservations" (Di Domenico, 2001, p.39). And again: "I am convinced in fact that only the learning library, the library that learns, will be in a position to create a proper heritage of knowledge and of evaluating it, enriching it and rennovating it." (Di Domenico, 2001, p.43).

The Role of Organizational Structures in Quality Control

> While it may be true that psychology as a whole has paid little attention to the world of things, the same cannot be claimed for engineering psychology and ergonomics which exclusively address the problems of man and his work environment, the interaction between man and machine, man and technology. However, it appears that in these disciplinary contexts we face another danger—a preoccupation with the individual and his or her work environment at the expense of neglecting its social implications: the danger of an individualistic myopia. (Ruiz Quintanilla, 1987, p.125)

Economic theorists recognize the correlation between institutional structures and economic performance, but as Wood and Frynas (2006) note, "there has been a glaring lack of research on institutional configurations which impede rather than promote economic success." (p. 240). The same could be said of research on institutional and organizational structures in libraries: success stories abound but failures, when they are not triumphantly declared to be successes, are discreetly passed over in silence. Wood and Frynas suggest that "institutional nestedness is the key building block of national economic success" (p. 240) and argue that segmented systems "characterized by rigid internal divisions between different areas of economic activity ... are likely to remain locked in a cycle of generally poor and uneven economic performance." (p. 239). While I do not intend to apply their reasoning and arguments to libraries, I do think that there are parallels (e.g. outsourcing; specialization of professionals into bibliographers, catalogers and public services; the division of labor within cataloging between professionals/original cataloging and nonprofessionals/copy-cataloging); at the very least the possibility that there are "institutional configurations which impede rather than promote" success should be investigated.

The impact of policies such as those mentioned above are not limited to the individual libraries implementing those policies, nor are these policies implemented without significant implications for organizational structures and the distribution of tasks. Many writers on cooperation and outsourcing (e.g. Skipper, 1967; Górny, 1994) have looked toward the benefits, but did not forsee the problems noted in Bland (1986), Stankowski (1990), Sapori (1995), Duke (1997), Hill (1998), Bade (2003) and Beall and Kafadar (2004) since they approached cooperation and outsourcing as purely technical possibilities. In shared databases, every institution's decisions effect every participating institution. Misinformation or the lack of information in a record input by one institution is more often than not accepted and reproduced rather than corrected by other institutions since the existence of "a bibliographic record" triggers a set of procedures which are enacted without regard to the accuracy, adequacy or usefullness of the record, and in many institutions these procedures call for routing the book through staff instructed to "pass it on" with neither review nor correction. Below minimal records input by prestigious libraries are copied and sometimes "enhanced" to PCC FULL/Core (or LC) and returned to the shared database apparently without any examination of the item's contents, and thereafter libraries see not the below minimal level coding but coding for PCC or LC even though the misinformation has not been changed. Scrutiny for accuracy and evaluation for adequacy are often abandoned or made the responsibility of an external agency (e.g. MARS for batch authority processing) since it is assumed that the records acquired (from whatever source) are the work of professionals and therefore acceptable. In this organizational scheme for the creation of catalogues we find outsourcing (for that is what copy-cataloging is in essence), division of labour (professional/original vs. nonprofessional/copy catalogers; creation vs. maintenance), distributed/unclear responsibilities (cooperation, shared databases/networks), automation in an increasingly complex system, and all of these appear over again in the work of catalogue maintenance. Any one of these organizational elements if not carefully initiated, overseen and continually evaluated in relation to the other elements of the system can create havoc; the combination of these processes can easily lead to results that escape any local or even international awareness and control.

    Technological developments have led many librarians—not just administrators—to imagine and investigate the potential for using these technologies and the networks in which they are imbedded to fundamentally alter and thereby improve the workflow in libraries, from acquisitions to cataloging to document delivery. The necessity of understanding the wider environment and relationships in any such reorganization through the exploitation of technologies has been clearly articulated in a recent article by Robertson and Barton (2005):

> The widespread realisation of the potential benefits of these differences for metadata workflow requires a model of the DIE [distributed information environment], which could facilitate strategic partnerships, inform divisions of labour and funding, and foster a holistic approach to the creation, augmentation and enhancement of metadata. To achieve this two conditions must be met: firstly, the local workflow must be articulated; and secondly this local workflow must be placed in the context of the wider environment, so that its relationship with other relevant workflows can be understood and acted upon. (Robertson and Barton, 2005, p. 9)

Unfortunately it has all too often been the case that the proposals put forth for reorganizing cataloging departments have been narrowly conceived according to technical possibilities rather than as systems dependent upon that wider environment, both affecting and being affected by the multiple and complex relationships which exist in today's networks of libraries, databases and all of the organizations involved in the information, misinformation and technology industries. The results have sometimes been disastrous not only for the originating institution, but for the entire wider environment. It appears to be the case that many of the organizational elements mentioned above lead to a multitude of problems, each entailing another in its turn. Probably all of them can be linked to Ashby's Law of Requisite Variety (Ashby, 1956, p.206), which basically states that in order to maintain control of a system, the controller of the system must be in possession of as much variety as the system to be controlled. Certain systems of the division of labor such as LC's practice of providing description by someone with linguistic competence and subject analysis by someone with subject specialization but not necessarily any linguistic competence for any given item maintain that requisite level of variety within the institution, but cannot guarantee it at another level within the organization. Other systems such as outsourcing simply remove all requisite variety from the institution. In all such organizational structures, most things may well appear to move along fine but this appearance is due to the fact that the institutional capacity to notice when something goes wrong has been lost.

Karen Calhoun of Cornell University Library, one of the leading exponents of automation, deskilling and technologically driven change in libraries, recently remarked that "In the area of data management, the key trend driving all others is the shift from data entry—that is, working on records one by one—to data manipulation—that is, working on batches of records at once." (Calhoun, 2003, p.284). Two key but unstated assumptions in her article are that the data already exist and that neither data entry nor data manipulation involve knowledge, interpretation, understanding or judgement,[47] that data management does not involve the creation of data (information, knowledge) but simply the management of what already exists, "working on records"; were it otherwise, such a shift would be inconceivable. Unfortunately, information technologies presuppose the creation of meanings by purposive agents: there is no information "out there" that search engines can find and manipulate unless that information has been created by someone for some reason.[48]

Rather than look at the numerous organizational structures that can and often do lead to a reduction of quality in the catalogue and therefore in the service provided to the users, I shall examine the assumptions, results and ramifications of the reorganization of cataloging at Cornell University Library under Ms. Calhoun's direction and the policies implemented for and praised as an efficient solution to problems of the timeliness and productivity of cataloging: Cornell's LTS Procedure #53: Classification on Receipt.[49]

A Case Study: Classification on Receipt

In January 2003 Cornell University Library implemented a set of procedures called Classification on Receipt (hereafter, COR). The procedures outlined in COR are to be used for "printed monographic

---

[47] In an outstanding paper Bereijo (1999) provided excellent arguments and discussion of the exact opposite interpretation: "Right now, the human element continues being an essential factor as interpreter of the real world, transforming the perceived impressions into conceptual entities amenable to symbolic manipulation by computer. ... Descriptive cataloging ... is not a routine and mechanical activity, an unreflective transcription of bibliographical data, but a complex process of interpretation requiring of the cataloger a high degree of technical qualification and judgement necessary for continual decision making."

[48] Even the simple act of identifying the author of a work as the author in a bibliographical record involves the creation of information. For a brief discussion of some of the most fundamental aspects of information creation in cataloging see Innocenti (1984).

[49] A more extensive treatment of COR, comparing it with policies at Princeton and the University of Chicago may be found in Bade (2007b)

materials that, upon receipt, are ineligible for fast or copy cataloging and that are not immediately selected for original cataloging."[50] Original catalogers examine all incoming materials and select only non-monographic and high-priority monographic items for full original cataloging; everything else goes through the COR procedure. It is a local procedure that requires a complex network of external organizations all operating according to a more traditional model. Error correction, subject analysis and detailed, accurate description are all outsourced to commercial vendors. The vendors in turn do no evaluation of the information which they provide Cornell; their procedure is simply to search a database for bibliographic records containing coding indicating a certain level of completeness,[51] or check the data in certain fields against a file of authorized forms, and pass on what they find to their clients. Those bibliographical records and authorized headings may or may not have been created by persons capable of intelligently and accurately creating appropriate bibliographic information; the only real requirement for entering this information into bibliographic and authority files is institutional participation in certain cooperative databases and programs. In this network of working relationships it is clear that Cornell has relinquished all responsibility for the accuracy and completeness of their bibliographic information in the pursuit of faster and cheaper production. If everything everywhere beyond the boundaries of Cornell libraries were perfect, this system would work, at least as long as Cornell never received any materials that were not available and catalogued elsewhere; if Cornell produces COR records for unique items or if anything goes wrong anywhere, Cornell suffers the results and has no mechanism for discovering much less correcting the problems.

COR has a few significant but mostly unstated premises underwriting its implementation:

---

[50] All quotations unless otherwise noted are from Cornell Libraries CTS Procedures web page for LTS Procedure #53, viewed online 21 June 2006 at: http://www.library.cornell.edu/cts/53cor.htm

[51] No automated system and no human being without the item catalogued can determine the level of completeness of a bibliographic record without the item in hand; what can be checked is the fixed field indicating cataloging level. Without the item in hand, that code cannot be evaluated for appropriateness but must be accepted at face value.

1) rapid processing is the only goal;
2) quick decisions are better than intelligent decisions because they are quicker;
3) "COR records are, like input or vendor records, designed to be temporary";
4) the records are not intended for user access but for machine matching at a later date;
5) general keyword searching is the only search strategy which the record needs to support;
6) error correction and prevention are unimportant;
7) misinformation and the lack of information for an indefinite period of time are of no consequence or at least of less importance than shelving immediately;
8) others external to the institution will provide the necessary completion and corrections;
9) any additions and changes made by anyone anywhere will be both appropriate and adequate for local needs;
10) all other institutions will continue to operate in a more intelligent and responsible manner.

What is wrong with these assumptions? Hélène Denis offered a list of five reasons that catastrophes seem to come out of nowhere:

- Ignorance of the dangers that surround us;
- An incomplete analysis of the risks;
- A lax definition of acceptable risk;
- The complexity of major sociotechnical risk
- Inadequate measures of attention and preparation

(Denis, 2005, p.70)

The COR policy represents a spectacular example of all of these reasons for catastrophe in the building of an information system. Denis suggested that in the absence of actual catastrophes and evident risks, "prevention is often the impoverished parent" in governments and business alike, concluding her essay with the remark that it is "cooperation between professionals that defines the technologies and their reliability, these being not any preexisting reality but a provisional achievement" (p. 78), a conclusion that one can find in diverse formulations in numerous publications on high-reliability organizations.

Compare COR with the "hallmarks of High Reliability":

- Preoccupation with failure
- Reluctance to simplify interpretations
- Sensitivity to operations
- Commitment to resilience
- Deference to expertise

(Weick & Sutcliffe, 2001, p. 10)

In COR, the only failure that matters involves the technical process (Marcadia); the policy insists upon simplification of all interpretation and in many cases prefers no interpretation; the only sensitivity to operations indicated in the procedures is that the more likely materials are to be cataloged by others the more one may choose to process them as COR records; resilience is expected to come entirely as a result of the outsourcing operations for record upgrading and authority control; expertise is neither sought nor valued since the record is only intended to be a temporary record.

"The chief danger of modern media consists in subordinating our thought to its speed and brevity" Večerník suggested, and his interiewer responded that this is due "in every case to the failure of science and intelligence." (Večerník and Hvížďala, 2003, p.46-47) The COR procedures discussed below certainly lend credence to the opinions of Večerník and Hvížďala. The stress on speed and specific directives to limit thinking ("agonizing" as the Cornell administrators describe it), changing and correcting are present throughout the document and deserve some discussion.

"Do not fuss over them [i.e. COR records] extensively." The proper interpretation of "extensively" is implied in the remainder of the document: any activity that takes time (i.e. understanding, interpretation, considering the potential users, making judgements, correction) is too much fussing.

"[R]etain data elements that are already present in the record you are modifying unless they are clearly in error." "Do not delete or change information unless it is clearly inaccurate or egregiously misleading." In order to ascertain that something is "clearly in error" one must have a different understanding of what the correct information should be, an understanding that can only come from an examination of the item itself. While COR catalogers are instructed to pay attention to errors only if they are "clearly inaccurate or egregiously misleading," Marty (2005)

noted that "Tracking down and correcting even the simplest error helped them improve and evolve their information systems overall." (p.318). His final paragraphs present conclusions similar to that arrived at by philosophers of science and researchers on high reliability organizations:

> As this article has demonstrated, information systems encouraging error recovery have a much greater potential value than merely helping employees to correct the odd, unexpected error that sneaks through already existing error prevention mechanisms. By supporting and encouraging error recovery in collections databases, employers are actually supporting and encouraging a culture in which employees are rewarded for taking an active role in improving the quality of data across the entire organization. The attitude that there is no reason to bother correcting a small number of errors can breed an environment in which employees are more likely to look the other way when errors occur, even if they were in a position to correct those errors and regardless of the severity of the error or their desire to fix it. In contrast, the attitude that one should not let an opportunity to correct mistakes slide by, even knowing full well that correcting all mistakes is impossible, can encourage employees to improve data quality in collections databases and to believe that developing more robust information systems is a worthwhile goal to pursue.
>
> The implications of this article, therefore, are generalizable for all information organizations at multiple levels of implementation. First, they demonstrate how error recovery procedures, if properly implemented and encouraged in collections databases, can help the users of these systems play a role in detecting and correcting unexpected errors, which would solve a variety of problems for libraries, museums, and archives. Second, they document how collections databases that are flexible, open, and designed to work with errors tend to be more robust and more likely to encourage error recovery than systems that are rigid, closed, and designed to prevent errors. Finally, they illustrate how information organizations concerned with finding the best error management techniques for their collections databases will reap rewards that go beyond a simple ability to correct errors. (Marty, 2005, p. 323-324)

"Accept what is present to the extent possible..." The ultimate mark of conservatism. Given the emphasis on speed and the prohibition of thinking (fussing), the quickest and most efficient solution for the staff member is to accept everything just as it is.

"Limit changes." This, from the advocates of "radical change" in catalogue departments. A broad proscription such as this can only have an inhibiting effect on any desire to make sense of the record and the library catalogue.

"Do not agonize over which call number to choose if the series has been classed in more than one call number; make a quick judgment to select one that is appropriate for the item." Instead of using this conflict as an opportunity to learn why more than one class number has been assigned (and perhaps correcting a serious error), one simply makes a quick decision, thereby prohibiting both learning and error correction.

"Add English words, translated generally from the title, to items written in foreign languages... If the title field does not contain words about the subject of the work, quickly examine the covers, tables of contents, and preface to select appropriate words." The assumption here is that the title will usually indicate clearly and unambiguously the subject, i.e. that no investigation, analysis or interpretation is needed, only selecting a few words from a prominent source which will be combined in no meaningful way in an uncontrolled subject field (653).[52] In order to determine whether or not the title contains words descriptive of the contents, one must first have an understanding of what the contents are, i.e. one must look beyond the title *in every case*.

---

[52] In the Autocat archives for 5 Sept. 2006 one can find a splendid example of the inadequacy of title alone for determination of the subject and classification of a work. Erin Barta had written earlier: "I have a book needing original cataloging. It is entitled "Longing for a land : the story of a Persion woman's individuation in America." So, is this classified under Jungian psychology -- "individuation" being the keyword -- or women-iran-psychology, or Iranians-United States-Psychology. ..." Karen Gorss Benko's full reply: "If the author is a Jungian psychologist writing about individuation and using this woman as an illustrative case, then I would classify it with Jungian psychology. If the author *is* the Persian woman, and she is writing about her experience immigrating to the United States, then I would classify it with Persians/Iranians as an element in the US population, if there is such a category. If the author is the Persian woman, and she is writing about her travels as a foreign tourist/visitor in the US, then I would classify it with Persian/Iranian women, I guess. I could keep on dreaming up scenarios. Really hard to classify according to a title. Important questions: who is the author? who is the intended audience? In what sense is the word "individuation" used (Jung didn't patent it or anything, I'm guessing)?"

"*If it is not possible to determine useful words quickly, omit the 653.* **Do not analyze the book in depth nor agonize over selection of terms.*"* [Bold type in the original.] Note the repeated use of the word "agonize" to describe the work of information seeking, interpretation and judgement. If you cannot do the work mindlessly and quickly, then you should not do it for not doing it does not matter. Subject analysis is eliminated for precisely those items which are not readily amenable to title keyword access!

"*Do not duplicate a term that appears in another keyword-searchable field of the record.*" The assumption here is that a general keyword search is what the user will use, since any intelligent search will fail in this impoverished information environment. The effect of basing description upon this assumption is that the record created can *only* be retrieved on a general keyword search; all intelligent search strategies are defeated and rendered useless by this limitation of description. While LC's decision to cease the creation of controlled series headings resulted in rendering intelligent series searching counterproductive, COR renders all intelligent searching useless.

"*If the work is about a person, place or corporate body, give the name in direct order in the 653 field. For corporate names, make a quick judgment whether an English translation would provide useful keyword access (if not, omit it).*" Again, general keyword searching is assumed to be the sole manner of information seeking among the users, and intelligent searching (e.g. according to authorized forms) is rendered counter-productive. In one of the examples given in the COR document, the title *Historia del Sindicato de Culinarias* is given the 653 Culinary Syndicate, a heading which is presumably useful for subject access but which matches nothing which anyone would know to search for, it being not a variant name of the Sindicato but a literal translation made locally and, of course, quickly.

The result of this organization of the work of cataloging has been an extraordinary increase in productivity but increased productivity is not the only result, and productivity itself has been divorced from any qualitative dimensions: productivity has become synonymous with quantity. The results not only affect Cornell's library, but the catalogers who do the work, the international databases to which Cornell distributes its records, the libraries worldwide that use those databases, workflows within those libraries, and users everywhere of all kinds, not just librarians. Without pretending to be exhaustive, the following results have become clearly evident:

Classification/shelf browsing rendered meaningless

This result was discussed above in connection with policies elsewhere, but the COR policy deserves additional comment. The COR document states that the records are intended to be temporary, but in a later statement Banush made clear that the classification *is* permanent for all of these materials ("classification numbers will not be changed"—Banush, 2003). If Abbott (2006) is correct in insisting that browsing is "one thing that absolutely must be protected in the research libraries of the future," then COR has destroyed the one thing necessary.

Precise searching is counterproductive

Sawyer and Davis' (1984) conclusion remains sound: "Sophisticated search and retrieval capabilities are worthless if the data on which the searches depend are inaccurate" (p. 217). The combination of broad subject terms rather than precise terms, uncontrolled subject data that for non-English materials is largely restricted to translation of elements found in the title, the prohibition of duplicating information found in one field in another and the nonprovision of subjects in many cases, particularly where interpretation and judgement is required, severely reduces the value of all precise, intelligent searching, leaving the general keyword search as the only possibility when comprehensive retrieval is desired, that being in many cases impossible due to the lack of any information input for many items. This goes not only for users of Cornell libraries but for users of the shared databases as well, since these records are sent to the shared bibliographical utilities.

Creation and dissemination of misinformation

I have examined many COR records which have been tape-loaded to OCLC and from these it is clear that most if not all of these records are created using a constant data function, since the vast majority of them have identical information in most of the fixed fields, regardless of their applicability to the items themselves. Subject headings are, when present, frequently much too general to be useful or are in fact incorrect, but these, rather than an analysis of the item, nonetheless serve as the basis of much of the enhancing done to COR records by other libraries, including LC. The combination of using constant data macros and title keywords as subjects in order to save time with a policy of "Do not correct" results in the deliberate creation of misinformation which is then distributed globally via tapeload to the shared databases.

In "Observations on fraud and scientific integrity in a digital environment" LaFollette made the following remarks on the ethical relationship between publishers, editors and authors:

> First, as researchers, we want to be able to trust what we read in the journals in our field. With so much information published, in so many diverse and mutable forms, some type of certification or sifting—trustworthy and reliable certification or sifting—will become paramount. There must be increased attention, therefore, to ethical standards for validation and evaluation. ... Hapless readers subjected to an explosion of sloppy scholarship, multiple misspellings, and similar avoidable errors will soon demand that authors—and journals—pay more attention to such details. Authors have an ethical responsibility to be especially careful and conscientious in an electronic context, where errors can take on a life of their own. Even the mundane issue of citation takes on new importance in a world where semingly unlimited amounts of "useful" information is present on the Web in one week and moved to another address or changed altogether the next. (LaFollette, 2000, p.1336)

Should not the same ethical attitudes be expected of librarians?

Errors persist and propagate

In the previous paragraphs we noted that misinformation is deliberately created, but since COR records are not intended to be permanent, this misinformation is also considered to be temporary. However, Banush (2003) stated that "We currently have no plans to retrieve items from the stacks and upgrade them should they lack better copy after the 2-year Marcadia cycle," so in spite of the COR document's insistence that the records are intended to be temporary, the entire record for all COR items are effectively intended to be permanent *unless something better comes along within 2 years*. And of course the records for all unique items will be permanent. Finally, many of the upgrades performed in OCLC on the basis of these Cornell COR records treat them as essentially correct and simply add trivia and change the 653 tags into the appropriate 600, 610, 630, 650 or 651 without investigating the item or correcting the subjects supplied by Cornell. Numerous examples of these "enhanced" records are reproduced in full and discussed in Bade (2003; 2004).

Catalogue management and all corrective activity are removed from the library, and therefore all capacity for quality control and evaluation. No one can observe the decline of access because no one is looking at the obstacles to access since error correction is permitted only in "obvious" cases. Weick and Sutcliffe noted that being "preoccuppied with failures, large and mostly small" was a primary characteristic of HROs:

> HROs encourage reporting of errors, they elaborate experiences of a near miss for what can be learned, and they are wary of the potential liabilities of success, including complacency, the temptation to reduce margins of safety, and the drift into automatic processing. (Weick and Sutcliffe, 2001, p.10-11).

Encourages poor working habits, prohibits the exercise of scholarly values, destroys professionalism

Serbian librarians are asking "How to build a culture of quality into an organization's culture?" (Stokić, 2004, p.46) while American librarians are priding themselves on destroying organizational culture altogether. Catalogers are treated essentially like unskilled laborers and temporary workers, and Guerrini's remarks are appropriate in this context as well:

> An adequate number of qualified persons ensures a minimum of work time with optimal results. Libraries resort more and more to temporary personnel recruited through competitive and cooperative contracts. While the solution can be positive by favoring the introduction of younger persons to the world of work and by solving cataloging problems otherwise unsolvable, it becomes pernicious the moment when the library (or the body which oversees it) uses as the only criteria of selection the lowest price. The inevitable consequence is an unsatisfactory catalogue and inadequate economic treatment of the cataloger that is humiliating for the workers. The result of lower quality arises almost always from the need to reduce cataloging time ... a temporal restriction that results in frustration, because it prevents the expression of the cataloger's professional values. (Guerrini, 2002, p. 39-40)

Increased burden on other libraries

David Woods' First Law of Cooperative Systems: "It's not cooperation, if either you do it all or I do it all." (Woods and Hollnagel, 2006, p.117). Cooperative cataloging depends entirely upon the contributions of the cooperating libraries. COR records represent the refusal to contribute the institution's fair share, thus requiring other libraries to do Cornell's work for them, work that many libraries cannot afford to do: "Back in 1991-92, the head of technical services had us locking and upgrading K-level records for credit off the OCLC bill. ... but after a while it proved too time consuming for us and that practice was discontinued." (Donaldson, 2006). That other libraries cannot afford to correct and complete the work of Cornell and others leads to the result that all libraries continue to find the original deficient record rather than the enhanced record they hope or believe they should find.

Kills the goose that lays the golden eggs

Denis' remark quoted above identifies the principle problem, namely that it is "cooperation between professionals that defines the technologies and their reliability, these being not any preexisting reality but a provisional achievement" (Denis, 2005, p. 78). It is mutual dependability—not the technologies in themselves—that provides a constant successful outcome, a matter stressed by Weick and one which he illustrated with the examples of stable families and alcohol rehabilitation programs. Situations and systems founded upon mutual dependability "collapse when people stop doing whatever produced the stable outcome" (Weick, 1987, p. 119). Writing of joint human-computer systems Hollnagel (2002, p. 4) noted that "In any situation where humans use artefacts to accomplish something, the dependability of the artefact is essential. Quite simply, if we cannot rely or depend on the artefact, we cannot really use it." COR already presents great problems for many libraries; should other libraries adopt COR or similarly organize and instruct their cataloging departments, there will soon be no bibliographic information created, completed or corrected, much less shared, among libraries: the system in its entirety will collapse.

In the final analysis, the evaluation of COR must be even more damning than Preece and Fox's evaluation of LC's preliminary records: "An experiment designed to foster resource sharing had foundered because of its incompatibility with the needs of network members for a standardized and reliable cataloging source." (Preece and Fox, 1992, p.8). COR is not an experiment but a deliberately planned procedure designed to pick the pockets of other libraries and undermine resource sharing. And if that were not enough, it fails as a reliable method for information provision: no information in a COR record can be accepted by anyone as being accurate or adequate, i.e. COR records are neither trustworthy nor reliable.

Where Does Information Come From? Trust and Reliability as the Foundation of Database Quality

> The general category of quality, as a challenge or superordinate reference, lies in two concepts (in the manner of master criteria), which are: truth and trust. (Valles, 2005, p.110-111)

In 1997 Marcum observed that there had been a change in library education:

> Recognizing the changes that have been wrought by digital technology ...these information management programs stress the retrieval of information by individuals or by software to meet user needs. The emphasis is on discovery and retrieval of information; relatively little emphasis is given to content or collection building. The new-style schools seem to think that content is a given. (Marcum, 1997)

If we juxtapose Marcum's comment with the statement of Calhoun on the move from one-at-a-time cataloging to batch processing, we can see the key issue clearly: if content is a given—and not produced in and by the library—then the quality of that content is the responsibility of the producers/providers, not the library. It is this alone that makes it possible to consider batch processing of bibliographical data rather than the creation of bibliographical records one at a time. There can be no quality assessment of the database without an assessment of the individual records, and that assessment, as the least reflection will reveal, is only possible if one compares the bibliographic record to the item itself, an impossibility in batch processing.

Many librarians, library educators and library administrators believe that content already exists and is not nor needs to be created in libraries. Libraries are assumed to be institutions dedicated to information provision but **not** to the creation, evaluation and organization of knowledge or information. Even those who have written at length on misinformation and research fraud have to my knowledge never acknowledged the role of libraries in the creation of information/misinformation.[53] Many librarians, library educators and administrators neither recognize nor understand the severe limits of automatic methods of description, analysis and indexing and hence do not realize the *necessity* of information creation (interpretation, sense-making) in libraries. Which is to say that these librarians, library educators and administrators are dangerously ill-informed and out of touch with both the needs of information technologies and library users.

Karl Weick and his associates studied organizations that "share a singular demand: They have no choice but to function reliably." (Weick and Sutcliffe, 2001, p.xiii). What they found was not just the unique structural features that others had noticed but that "These organizations also think and act differently." (ibid.) They compared their observations with the University of Michigan's list of the forty five most pressing problems identified by business leaders and concluded: "What impressed us was that those forty-five problems, almost without fail, involved a lapse in reliability." (ibid, p.xiv) The managers of HROs were able to achieve high reliability because of "their uncommon success in finding ways to stay *mindful* about what is happening. They update their ideas of what is happening and are not trapped by old categories or crude renderings of the contexts they face. ... It takes *mindful variety* to assure stable high performance." (ibid. p.xv. Italics in the original).

What is mindfulness?

> Generally, mindfulness is expressed in active information processing, characterized by cognitive differentiation: the creation of categories and distinctions. The act of creating distinctions tacitly creates new categories and vice versa. The distinctions drawn may be judged to be major or minor, but they are mindfully drawn just the

---

[53] A recent example appeared in Marsh and Dibben's survey of the literature (English only, of course) on trust in information science and technology in which they noted that "ultimately the value and worthiness of that document and the information it contains are unknown unless the document is examined" (Marsh and Dibben, 2002, p.477) but they take for granted the value and worthiness of the metadata!

same. Mindfulness may be seen as creating (noticing) multiple perspectives, or being aware of context. When in this state, the person is becoming more and more differentiated while differentiating the external world. The entire individual is involved in creating. In contrast, in a mindless mode, the individual relies on categories that have already been formed and distinctions that have already been drawn. (Langer, 1989, p.138-139)

What is mindful variety? Perhaps an example of its opposite will suffice:

> SCC's [Software Consulting Company] workers ... become dependent, through training, socialization, and experience, on the productivity tools. Such actors lose the ability to reflect on the assumptions, rules, and concepts that facilitate and constrain their work. They lack conceptions of "how things could be otherwise" ... The dependence of consultants and the production process on the information technology may mean that the short-term gain in productivity and competitiveness afforded by the productivity tools could lead to SCC's long-term incapacity to respond flexibly to dynamic business conditions. Technology that mediates the production process of an organization is critical to the ongoing operations of the firm and hence strategic. A strategic technology, while it may be part of an organization's competitive initiative... may also be its key vulnerability. (Orlikowski, 1991, p.36)

The policies and structures examined above all involve a lapse in reliability, the removal of thought, judgement and responsibility from the persons creating, manipulating and maintaining the database, and hence from the library as a whole. Because it is assumed that the required information already exists or will be created elsewhere later, the quality, value and responsibility for the information is located externally. Since "The main source for believability is the author or creator of the information" (Naumann and Rolker, 1999), identifying the creators of information is important for judging information quality. When information is acquired from external sources, determining the reliability of the source is critical, but

> this cannot be done automatically. First, a user defined mapping of authors to believability scores must be created. Obviously this mapping is very subjective and must be newly created for each user. ... Also, one must assume that information sources will be very resourceful trying to find ways to improve believability without improving the correctness of the information itself. (Naumann and Rolker, 1999)

Because the work performed in the library is by policy not to be concerned with any of these issues of quality, complete trust has been placed in the technical system and all sources from which information may be acquired at any point in the process. The result is that the library no longer has any possibility of maintaining a mindful awareness of what is happening and loses the internal variety required to deal with the complexity of the system in its entirety. Compare the instructions for COR cataloging ("Accept what is present to the extent possible" etc.) with the remarks by Marsh and Dibben:

> If we are told something in an electronic world, how can we trust it? Previously, a document's credibility was to some extent maintained by knowledge workers such as librarians, editors, and other intermediaries. Today, this front line of information authentification is not always in place. The problem is compounded when one considers that searching for information may be done not by humans but by automated agents. (Marsh and Dibben, 2003, p.484-485)

Trusting external sources of metadata assumes that the ends for which those sources create information are compatible with the uses of that metadata in libraries. In the case of bibliographic information created by booksellers, that compatibility exists only in the case of the selector, and then only partially. Booksellers describe books in order to sell them, and this may lead to the inclusion of much information which may make distinguishing one edition from others difficult, the non-inclusion of information which might lead libraries not to purchase the item, different systems of transliteration, information from many sources included without indication of source, inclusion of prepublication information no longer accurate, and many other matters which are presumably not a problem for the bookseller but which can cause serious problems for the bibliographer, reference librarian and library users of all sorts. The following example of a record created by the book vendor Eastview and found in the OCLC database should sufficiently illustrate the problem.

```
LDR  nam Ma
001  62203556
005  20051102050328.1
008  051018suuuu   ru       000 0 rus d
040  EVIEW $b eng $c EVIEW
020  9994362828 : $c USD31.95
0290 EVIEW $b J2001627
049  CGUA
1001 Varfri, M.
24500Fjalor lokucionesh Frengjisht-Shqip = $b French – Albanian Idioms
Dictionary / $c Varfri, M.
260  Tirana : $b Albatros, $c [2000?]
300  256 p. ; $c cm.
546  In Russian $b (roman)
65004Humanities.
65004Languages/linguistics.
65004Albania.
```

Compare this "metadata" with what appears in the book received from Eastview as fulfillment of an order placed using that Eastview order record:

```
Language of the book: French entries, Albanian definitions;
        in the OCLC record's fixed fields: rus; 546: In Russian (roman)
Contents of the book: it is a dictionary;
        in OCLC fixed fields: no contents information given;
        subject fields:    650 humanities/languages/Albania
Title in the book: Fjalor lokucionesh frëngjisht-shqip [and nothing else];
        in OCLC 245:  Fjalor lokucionesh Frengjisht-Shqip = French-
        Albanian idioms
        dictionary
Statement of authorship in the book: Nonda Varfi, Viktor Z. Bakillari;
        in OCLC: 245 / Varfri, M.; 100 Varfri, M.
Imprint in the book: place of pub: Tiranë;
        in OCLC fixed fields: ru [Russia]; in 260: Tirana
Date of publication in the book: t.p. verso c2004;
        in OCLC Fixed fields: date uuuu; 260: [2000?]
Pagination in the book: 252 p.;
        in OCLC 300: 256 p.
```

The vendor's metadata and the vendor's book received on that order ought to match, yet the only fields in the entire record which are both present and correct are the ISBN and the publisher's name, Albatros. Every other field/subfield is either missing, contains errors or is completely wrong. For a bibliographer who does not know Albanian, the English translation may be useful and perhaps for this reason it was entered into the record. But for the bibliographer, cataloger, researcher who has a citation to the actual book, it may well appear that the item described by the bookseller is a different edition, and if searched by author or qualified by date or language, it will not be found at all. The cataloger and the acquisition librarian alike are forced to ask an unanswerable question: did we in fact receive what we ordered or something different?

Once reliability is seriously questioned, trust is impossible and the entire system collapses: the database in its entirety is suspect and no longer usable. Those who continue to trust in the system do so only because they no longer have any mindful awareness of what is happening.

IV. Policy and Politics

The nature of library databases and catalogues will depend upon the ideas and attitudes which inform the labours of their creators, and therefore always a matter of policy. The quality of those databases may be judged differently by the creators, the managers and the various users. The more one is in control of the creation of the data, the more one can determine its quality. The problem for users is that they can praise or complain, but if they are not in control of the creation, then there is little they can do about quality as they assess it.

In academic libraries the principle users—those for whose purposes alone the library exists—are not the creators of the databases and catalogues which are at their disposal. The responsibility for the quality as determined by researchers' needs is delegated to librarians. When those librarians outsource the creation of their databases and catalogues to external organizations, they have lost all control over the process: they have relinquished responsibility. Ill-informed beliefs in technological promises and trust in the information/misinformation industries has led many librarians to cast their responsibility to the winds:

> [T]he machine like the djinnee, which can learn and can make decisions on the basis of its learning, will in no way be obliged to make such decisions as we should have made, or will be acceptable to us. For the man who is not aware of this, to throw the problem of his responsibility on the machine, whether it can learn or not, is to cast

his responsibility to the winds, and to find it coming back seated on the whirlwind. ... When human atoms are knit into an organization in which they are used, not in their full right as responsible human beings, but as cogs and levers and rods, it matters little that their raw material is flesh and blood. What is used as an element in a machine, is in fact an element in the machine. Whether we entrust our decisions to machines of metal, or those machines of flesh and blood which are bureaus and vast laboratories and armies and corporations, we shall never receive the right answers to our questions unless we ask the right questions. (Wiener, 1956, p. 185-186)

Perhaps the most intelligent and clearly articulated discussion of the state of libraries in the early 21st century was published by Wendell Berry in 1977. Even though the book was not about libraries at all but about agriculture, and in spite of having been written thirty years ago, his description and interpretation of farming/library ecologies remains unmatched in the farming/library literature. His book chronicled a history of policies based on naive understandings of technological developments and the possibilities and promises associated with them, followed by the effects of the implementation of those policies on local farm ecologies, economies, social networks and the transmission of working, specialized, locally adapted cultural knowledge that enabled farming communities to maintain themselves. A focus on productivity which ignored all other aspects of the natural and social ecology of farming led to the government slogan "Get big or get out!," policies, it should be remembered, that were developed and enforced not by farmers or anyone involved in farming but by government administrators and university academics, both equally out of touch with farming as a practice.

"The enormous productivity of industrial agriculture cannot be denied, but neither can its enormous ecological, economic, and human costs, which are bound eventually to damage its productivity" wrote Berry (1996, p.230) in the Afterword to the 3rd edition of his book. The results of those policies exactly parallel later developments in libraries, continuing into our time: financial squeezes brought about by the costs of upgrading and maintaining equipment that is constantly becoming obsolete, the loss or destruction of the tools and knowledge which would enable the discovery or implementation of any alternative methods, depopulation of farming communities leading to the necessity of migrant laborers (outsourcing) or yet more machinery and the consequent increase in debt, and the transformation of a meticulous caring of local places and all their natural populations into the industrial exploitation of acreage by large farm corporations for the sole purpose of extracting a profit. The requisite variety that a place, a community and a practice requires was destroyed, as were the communities themselves.

This has happened in libraries, and continues apace.[54] When the values and practices of science and scholarship—evidence, accuracy, checking for error, argumentation, truth—have been eliminated from the library it can indeed continue its existence as a group of managers overseeing an information proletariat, but can it serve the needs of a community whose values it repudiates *in toto*? When the work of libraries is assumed not to involve the building and managing of a collection for the particular needs of a particular community then the work can be performed mechanically or outsourced to the lowest bidder *because the results do not matter.*

Academic libraries have one reason for existing: to serve the needs of science and scholarship. To do that it is necessary to understand those practices and the values which unite the communities of scientists and scholars. And those which divide them:

> A recent clash between Management and Agricultural Economics faculty members at Purdue University over the continuing availability of print resources in their library illustrates the division (and at times divisiveness) in modern information-seeking practices. Management faculty argue that they have access to everything they need electronically and that their students don't use the books, "nor do we want them to." Agricultural economics faculty view removing the stacks as a "scholarly disaster." "We expect [students] to go back in history to see what's been said on the topic. But that's impossible to do with electronic resource because few older books have been digitized" (Kiernan, 2000). These two faculties, which share common library space, disagree about the survival of print in the digital revolution. ... Such differing perceptions about information resources and information needs in the digital age challenge certain fundamental values in librarianship. Ranganathan's second law, "Every reader his (or her) book," is clearly at risk not only at Purdue but in any library in which hard choices must be made about allocating information resources." (Diamond and Dragich, 2001, p. 410)

---

[54] Brief discussions may be found in Bereijo (1999), Bade (2002) and Revelli (2004).

Much of the existing debate over what constitutes quality in databases and catalogues betrays not only a lack of awareness of the diverse needs of science and scholarship but a repudiation of the core values of those practices: attention, observation, documentation, analysis, argumentation, verification, critique, probing for error, responsibility and accountability. All of these characteristics of academic research have been abolished from the library in the case of outsourcing, mindless copy-cataloging, original cataloging in the manner of Cornell's COR practices, and in any and all systems which relegate description, analysis and interpretation to an automated process, whether the automation is technological or bureaucratic.

The repudiation of academic values in libraries has not been limited to the organization of catalogue departments. Numerous publications, policies and institutional reorganizations have recently proposed and implemented top-down changes in libraries with a complete disregard for the opinion of those professionals most familiar with and involved in the work affected by the changes. Plans laid in secret, the refusal to invite much less accept professional opinion, silencing of dissent, scandalously inadequate research to support desired policies, and a refusal to look at the results of policies already enacted.[55] The Library of Congress' recent decision to discontinue making series authorities was surrounded from beginning to end with all of these anti-academic (and anti-democratic) practices.[56] One reads for example the following comments by David Banush of Cornell, inspired by LC's series treatment decision:

> The more conservative forces, which seem to include many front-line staff, are vigorously (sometimes stridently) defending the status quo, or even the status quo ante; others, primarily managers and administrators, are trying to move away from the old models toward something very different. ... Like many political and business leaders in Europe, most library leaders have identified the problems

---

[55] When confronted by yours truly with a number of heinously incorrect PCC records from Cornell in early 2003, David Banush responded with the comment that those records demonstrated acceptable differences of catalogers' judgement.
[56] See Mann (2006b), congressional testimony on the changes, and other papers available at guild2910.org. The origin of the present essay is rooted in a letter written in response to LC's series treatment decision (Bade, 2006a, reprinted in this volume).

and know what needs to be done, at least generally. But they also realize that for the most part, the staff do not want change. (David Banush, letter to PCCPOL, 24 May 2006)

Having identified library management (not those involved in the work) as those understanding the problems and being in possession of the knowledge of what needs to be done, and staff as those who "do not want change," Mr Banush continues with an outrageously patronizing hypocrisy:

> My unsolicited advice ... is not to fall into the trap of arguing with the people most threatened by change. ... Instead, I think that the PCC leadership should think carefully about what kinds of roles catalogers will have in the future. They need to gather feedback, listen closely, and allow for open discussions to take place. A genuine dialogue must occur; if the opinions are solicited only to be ignored, the process will be nothing more than a cynical facade, and it will most certainly backfire. If front-line folks feel they are part of the planning process, they may be much less likely to resist and much more likely to become engaged. We must also remember that in looking to the future, the past must be honored and respect [sic]. ... Honoring the past does not mean living in it, nor does it mean squandering opportunities for the future to placate the disgruntled staff of the present. ... It's obvious that library leaders who seek meaningful changes in the way we work have their work cut out for them. What is not so easy to see is how to bridge the gap between those who wish to move to a different way of looking at cataloging and catalogs and those who feel too threatened by change to consider reforms anything but heresy or betrayal. ... I believe Joan Swanekamp has pointed out that the strategic plan calls for PCC to assist catalogers in this time of transition. (ibid.)

It is difficult to see how one can speak of gathering feedback, listening closely and engaging in "genuine dialogue" when those leading the discussion are assumed to know it all already and those whose feedback is being solicited, those to be engaged in dialogue, are described as "the people most threatened by change," "disgruntled staff" and "those who feel too threatened by change to consider reforms." Instead of encouraging argument and debate as befits the academic community, managers are warned to avoid that "trap"—as befits an illegitimate power elite.

Similar contradictions appear in the writings of Karen Calhoun. For example not long after the COR procedures were implemented under her direction at Cornell, an article of hers appeared with the following closing paragraph:

> Technology is not the key to productivity in technical services, although it plays an important role and developing technological innovations is a critical ingredient. People are the key to success, together with what they know, their attitudes and their behaviors, how they choose to do their work, the tasks to which they are assigned, and the processes they use. Technical services departments can dramatically boost their productivity, provided they are willing to continually examine what they are doing, what they need to do, and how they do it. A graduated, increasingly skilled use of information technology, together with resourcefulness and creativity, can be the engine of momentous advances in library technical services. (Calhoun, 2003, p.288)

How can policies which forbid thinking, judgement and interpretation, which prohibit staff from examining "what they are doing, what they need to do, and how they do it" and in which there is no place for "resourcefulness and creativity" be the result of such praiseworthy attitudes? The reason is because all of this wonderful thinking, judgement, resourcefulness and creativity is reserved for library managers. The professionals who are responsible for creating the databases and catalogs, those "people most threatened by change" are merely "disgruntled staff... who feel too threatened by change to consider reforms" and therefore policy "debates" must ignore their objections.

Who is going to decide what the meaning of quality is for academic libraries?[57] Who is going to ensure that the level of quality in our cata-

---

[57] A currently fashionable argument against the collaborative labor of "disgruntled staff" (i.e. librarians devoted to catalogue and database creation, maintenance and coherence) is that whatever database creation, maintenance and coherence is needed can be and even ought to be produced by the free collaborative labor of "users" who would cost the library nothing. For example, a wikified catalogue could "build individual contributions into collective, synergistic projects without intervention from formal institutions or dependence on convenital expertise." (Duguid, 2006). However, Duguid argues that the success of some well known forms of collaborative labor such as Open Source software development has been dependent upon the self-selecting skills and knowledge that these activities require, the severe constraints of compatibility with existing tools (code), and usually the control and authority of the developers and maintainers of the project. Questions of quality, he writes "are less about what single source to trust for everything than

logues and databases is appropriate for any particular institution's users? Those who have an active commitment to and engagement with scholarship or those who believe that the task of the librarian is simply management of the information given? It is the position of the present author that the repudiation within libraries of the values and commitments of science and scholarship—attention, observation, accuracy, analysis, probing for error, argumentation, verification, criticism of presuppositions, assumptions, methodologies and results: in short, mindfulness, trust and truth—cannot lead to libraries which reliably serve science or scholarship. A wealth of evidence already exists that the mindlessness of cataloging as found in many research libraries combined with an uncritical trust in technological possibilities that can only be described as religious fanaticism is producing and distributing misinformation at an alarming rate. The advocates of this new way of doing things call this "the more expansive view of quality" (Banush, 2001). Something we should expect when science and scholarship, along with mindfulness, trust and truth have been banished from the library.

V. Conclusion

In spite of technological advances through the centuries, the problem of determining quality remains exactly as it always has been: What are the purposes of the institution? For what users and uses does the institution exist? Quality is always a local question, local in the sense of a defined set of users and uses rather than any users and all

---

about when to trust a particular source for the question at hand ... and when not?" He continues with the following remarks: "To fulfill the potential of peer production, we must first become more reflective or self-critical. We need a better understanding of the connection between the means of production and the quality of the outcome, to be aware of the likely strengths and possible weaknesses of different approaches, to consider why a method works when it does, and to become constructively critical of systemic weaknesses when it does not." (ibid.) These remarks are appropriate not only for the peer production of those masses presumably guided by the Hidden Hand common to advocates of capitalist and technological utopias (an ideological conjunction deliberately reflected in the title of Yochai Benkler's 2006 book *The Wealth of Networks*) but equally to the peer production of professional librarians guided by their open handed devotion to public service, learning and scholarship.

possible uses. Database quality is important to many people for many different reasons, and therefore judgements concerning quality do not necessarily retain their validity accross user groups. In a shared bibliographical database such as OCLC, no users can expect nor do they have the right to expect anything other than conformity to the miminal demands of the database managers and the requirements of the technical system. Any different desires or needs of users must be addressed at the local institutional level where those user purposes and practices are established as determining factors in the use of a database. This requires of each institution a familiarity with and understanding of the practices which the institution supports, a clear understanding of the various available means for supporting those practices, and decisions about which means the institution can afford to pursue.

In the case of academic libraries the practices of science, research and scholarship must be supported, and these not merely at the elementary level but with a clear understanding of the ideals and values that have shaped and continue to shape those practices at their highest level. The matter does not end there, however, for academic institutions are dedicated to learning and teaching, and these activities with all of their goals must also shape the work of the librarian. If progress in libraries and librarianship is not to be limited to technological change and responses to the same, if librarianship itself is to grow and develop as a professional practice, then librarianship should involve the discovery, creation, elaboration, criticism and teaching of the entire range of practices in library research, with a goal of providing library users with a knowledge of possible, adequate, useful, sufficient, efficient and thorough library research practices, demonstrating the best practices for each specific type of search and research activity. Furthermore, in the spirit of critical inquiry which has been the chief justification for science as a social practice, academic librarians ought to be critically examining and evaluating technologies and research practices in libraries in light of the goals and values of science and scholarship. What we find instead is the abandonment and even repudiation of all of the goals, values and practices of science and a positivistic academic librarianship uncritically following and supporting the predominant information seeking practices and beliefs of the larger society. Instead of maintaining libraries as a driving force for learning and the increase of knowledge we are being urged to become managers of an industrial process, securing status and power through slavishly following technological developments rather than intelligently using them and shaping their development through critical engagement. What is at stake in libraries is not simply the future direction of libraries, but the meaning of science and scholarship as social practices, perhaps even the continued existence of those practices. Whether we continue to serve the goals of science and scholarship or repudiate them will be evident in the policies we implement in our libraries today.

VI.   Bibliography

Abbott, Andrew (2006). *The University Library.* Available at: http://www.lib.uchicago.edu/staffweb/groups/space/abbott-report.html#VIA

Access Level Record for Serials Working Group Final Report July 24, 2006. Available at: http://www.loc.gov/acq/conser/alrFinalReport.html

Altick, Richard D. (1975). *The art of literary research.* New York: Norton.

Aracil, Lluís V. (1965/1982). "Conflicte lingüístic i normalització lingüística a l'Europa nova" in his *Papers de sociolingüística,* p.23-38. Edició i presentació a cura d'Enric Montaner. Barcelona: Edicions de la Magrana.

Armstrong, C.J. (1994). "Databases and quality: why not try 'What you see is what you get'?" *Managing information* v. 1 nr.11/12 (Nov.-Dec.) p.28-30.

Arnold, Stephen E. (1992). "Information manufacturing: the road to database quality" *Database,* October 1992, p.32-39.

Ashby, W. Ross (1956). *An introduction to cybernetics.* London: Chapman & Hall. Available at: http://pcp.vub.ac.be/books/IntroCyb.pdf

Babb, Nancy (2006). "Bibliography versus auto-bibliography: tackling the transformation of traditions in the research process." *Law library journal,* v.98 nr.3 p.451-480.

Bade, David (2002). *The creation and persistence of misinformation in shared library catalogs: language and subject knowledge in a technological era.* Urbana: GSLIS.

Bade, David (2003). *Misinformation and meaning in library catalogs.* Chicago: D. Bade.

Bade, David (2004). *The theory and practice of bibliographic failure, or, Misinformation in the information society.* Ulaanbaatar: Chuluunbat.

Bade, David (2006a). Letter posted to Autocat, 31 May 2006. Available at the Music Library Association Clearinghouse: http://library.music.indiana.edu/tech_s/mla/Bade_letter_May_0 6_.htm

Bade, David (2006b). "Report: Access Level cataloging of serials." Posting to Autocat July 26, 2006. Reprinted in: *Catapult,* issue 53, August 2006, p.5-6. Available at: http://www.lianza.org.nz/community/cat-sig/files/catapult_53.pdf

Bade, David (2007a). "Colorless green ideals in the language of bibliographic description: making sense and nonsense in the library." *Language & communication* v.27 nr.1 (January 2007) p.54-80.

Bade, David (2007b). "Rapid cataloging: three models for addressing timeliness as an issue of quality in library catalogs" *Cataloging & classification quarterly,* v.45, nr.1 (October) p.87-123

Bainbridge, Lisanne (1987). "Ironies of automation." In: J. Rasmussen et al. *New technology and human error,* p. 271-283.

Balaban, Oded (1998). "The use of error as an argument in the language of human sciences: the dogmatic use of error" *Semiotica* v.120 nr.1/2 p.139-159.

Banush, David (2001). *BIBCO Core Record study: final report prepared for the PCC Policy Committee.* Available at: http://www.loc.gov/catdir/pcc/bibco/coretudefinal.html

Banush, David (2003). Posting to PCCLIST, 21 July 2003.

Banush, David (2006). Posting to PCCPOL, 24 May 2006.

Beall, Jeffrey; Kafadar, Karen (2004). "The effectiveness of copy cataloging at eliminating typographical errors in shared bibliographic records" *Library resources and technical services,* v.48 nr.2 p.92-101.

Beaudiquez, Marcelle (1991). "Nouvelles techniques, nouvelle normalisation: une évolution pour de nouveaux besoins." In: Herman Liebaers et Marc Walckiers, eds., *Library automation and networking,* p.194-205.

Benko, Karen Gorss (2006). "Class for psychology." Autocat archives for 5 Sept. 2006.

Bereijo, Antonio (1999). "La catalogación descriptiva: aspectos que intervienen en la calidad procesual" *Revista Interamericana de Bibliotecología* v.22 no.1 (Jan-June) p.99-125.

Berger, Franz; Kempf, Klaus, eds. (2001). *Riforma universitaria e rivoluzione dei media: una sfida per le biblioteche universitarie: atti del convegno internazionale a Bolzano,* 28-29 settembre 2000. Fiesole: Casalini.

Berry, Wendell (1996; orig. 1977). *The unsettling of America: culture & agriculture.* 3rd ed. San Francisco: Sierra Club Books.

Bierly, Paul E. III; and Spender, J.-C. (1995). "Culture and high reliability organizations: the case of the nuclear submarine" *Journal of management* v.21 nr.4 p.639-656.

Blair, David C. (1990). *Language and representation in information retrieval.* Amsterdam; New York: Elsevier Science Publishers.

Blair, David C. (2003). "Information retrieval and the philosophy of language." *Annual Review of Information Science and Technology* v.37, p.3-50.

Bland, Robert N. (1986). "Quality control in a shared online catalog database: the Lambda experience" *Technical services quarterly* v.4 nr.2 (Winter) p.43-58.

Buehler, Helen (2007). Re: [ACAT] Qualifying headings. Posting to Autocat, 31 August 2007.

Byrd, Jackie, et al. (2006). *A white paper on the future of cataloging at Indiana University, January 15, 2006.* Available at:

http://www.iub.edu/~libtserv/pub/Future_of_Cataloging_White_Paper.pdf

Calhoun, Karen (2003). "Technology, productivity and change in library technical services" *Library collections, acquisitions, & technical services* v.27 p.281-289.

Calhoun, Karen (2006). *The changing nature of the catalog and its integration with other discovery tools. Final report, March 17 2006.* Available at: http://www.loc.gov/catdir/calhoun-report-final.pdf

Callon, Michel; Méadel, Cécile; Rabeharisoa, Vololona. (2000). "L'économie des qualités" *Politix* v.13 no52 p.211-239.

Capurro, Rafael (1990). "Towards an information ecology." In: Irene Wormell, ed., *Information quality: definitions and dimensions: proceedings of a NORDINFO seminar,* Royal School of Librarianship, Copenhagen, 1989. London: Taylor Graham, p.122-139.

Chauveinc, Marc (1983). "La ronde infernale: de la bibliographie à l'accès au document" in G. Varet, (ed.), *Bibliographie et informatique : les disciplines humanistes et leurs bibliographies à l'âge de l'informatique : table ronde du CNRS,* Besançon, 19 et 20 novembre 1982. Paris : Editions de la Maison des sciences de l'homme. (Travaux du Centre de documentation et bibliographie philosophiques de l'Université de Franche Comté), p.131-135.

Chauvin, Sophie; Papy, Fabrice (2005). "Peut-on déranger le bibliothécaire à la banque d'accueil?" Available at: http://www.caisacsi.ca/proceedings/2005/chauvin_2005.pdf

Chazal, Gérard (2003). "La mise en réseaux des savoirs." In: Pierre Musso, ed., *Réseaux et société.* Paris: PUF, p.119-137.

Clark, Philip M. (1990). "The micro edge: what cost accuracy?" *The Bottom Line,* v. 4 no.2 p.35-37.

Debril, Thomas (2005). "Le marché et la qualité. In: Minguet and Thuderoz (eds.), *Travail, entreprise et société: manuel de sociologie pour ingénieurs et scientifiques.* Paris: PUF, 192-209.

La démarche de qualité. (1998). Special issue of *Bulletin des bibliothèques de France,* t. 43 no.1.

Denis, Hélène (2005). "Les risques et les catastrophes" In: Minguet and Thuderoz (eds.), *Travail, entreprise et société: manuel de sociologie pour ingénieurs et scientifiques.* Paris: PUF, p.68-80.

Derfert-Wolf, Lidia; Bednarek-Michalska, Bożena, eds. (2000). *Międzynarodowa konferencja Zarządzanie przez jakość w bibliotece akademickiej Bydgoszcz*—Gniew, 10-13 wrzesnia 2000 r. Warszawa: Stowarzyszenie Bibliotekarzy Polskich, KWE. Available at: http://ebib.oss.wroc.pl/matkonf/atr/indexpl.html

Di Domenico, Giovanni (1999). "L'obiettivo e la pratica della qualità in biblioteca: brevi riflessioni sul contesto italiano" *Culture del testo,* no.13 (genn.-apr.), p.5-13.

Di Domenico, Giovanni (2001). "La biblioteca apprende: qualità organizzativa e qualità di servizio nella società cognitiva." In: O. Foglieni, ed., *La qualità nel sistema biblioteca,* p. 32-48.

Diamond, Randy; Dragich, Martha (2001). "Professionalism in librarianship: shifting the focus from malpractice to good practice" *Library trends,* v.49 no.3 (Winter), p. 395-414.

Donaldson, Bob Mead (2006). "Original cataloging of videos" posted to Autocat, 28 August 2006.

Dörner, Dietrich (1990). "The logic of failure" *Philosophical transactions of the Royal Society of London. Series B, Biological sciences,* v. 327, no. 1241, Human factors in hazardous situations (Apr. 12, 1990), p. 463-473.

Dörner, Dietrich (1997). *The logic of failure: recognizing and avoiding error in complex situations.* Reading, Mass: Addison-Wesley. Translation of Die Logik des Mißlingens.

Douglas, Mary; Ney, Steven (1998). *Missing persons: a critique of the social sciences.* Berkeley: University of California Press; New York: Russell Sage Foundation.

Duclos, Denis (1989). *La peur et le savoir: la société face à la science, la technique et leurs dangers.* Paris: La Découverte.

Duguid, Paul (2006). "Limits of self-organization: peer production and "laws of quality." *First Monday,* v. 11, no.10 (October 2006).

Duke, John Kenneth (1997). "Acceptable copy: quality in record selection and outsourcing: a report" *Library acquisitions* v.21 no.4 (Winter) p.483-485.

Dupuy, Jean-Pierre (1980). "Analyse de systèmes et critique de la société 'informationnelle.'" In: F. Gallouedec-Genuys, ed., *Les enjeux culturels de l'informatisation.* Fontefraud: Centre Culturel de l'Ouest. p. 183-201.

English, Larry P. (2005). "Information quality: critical ingredient for national security" *Journal of database management* v.16 nr.1 p.18-32.

Erbolato-Ramsey, Christiane; Grover, Mark L. (1994). "Spanish and Portuguese online cataloging: where do you start from scratch?" *Cataloging & classification quarterly* v.19 nr.1 p.75-87.

Eymard-Duvernay, François (1989). "Conventions de qualité et formes de coopération" *Revue économique* v.40 no.2 p.329-359.

Fabietti, Ettori (1933). *La biblioteca pubblica moderna.* Milano: A. Vallardi.

Fernández-Molina, J. Carlos (1995). "La responsabilidad de los profesionales de la documentación en la prestación de servicios de información" *Revista española de documentación científica* v.18 nr.3 p.320-332.

Foglieni, Ornella, ed. (2001). *La qualità nel sistema biblioteca: innovazione tecnologica, nuovi criteri di gestione e nuovi standard di servizio.* Milano: Editrice bibliografica.

Freon, Marie-Elise, ed. (1996). *Controler la qualité et la coherence d'un catalogue.* Villeurbanne: Institut de formation des bibliothecaires.

Fugmann, Robert (1994). "Galileo and the inverse precision/recall relationship: medieval attitudes in modern information science" *Knowledge organization* v.21 nr.3 p.153-154.

Fujita, Yushi; and Hollnagel, Erik (2004). "Failures without errors: quantification of context in HRA" *Reliability engineering and system safety* v.83 p.145-151.

Galileo Galilei (1960 [1623]). The Assayer. In: Galileo Galilei et al., *The controversy on the comets of 1618*. Translated by Stillman Drake and C.D. O'Malley. Philadelphia: University of Pennsylvania Press, p. 151-336.

Galli, Giovanni (2001). "L'utente senza qualità: divagazioni e numeri." In: O. Foglieni, ed., *La qualità nel sistema biblioteca*, p.239-253.

Ganińska, Halina (2000). "Jakość, koszty jakości i efektywność usług informacyjnych—elementy strategii ekonomicznej w bibliotece politechnicznej." In: Derfert-Wolf and Bednarek-Michalska, eds., *Międzynarodowa konferencja Zarządzanie przez jakość w bibliotece akademickiej Bydgoszcz*—Gniew, 10-13 wrzesnia 2000 r. Warszawa: Stowarzyszenie Bibliotekarzy Polskich, KWE. Available at: http://ebib.oss.wroc.pl/matkonf/atr/ganinska.html

Giappiconi, Thierry (2001). *Manuel théorique et pratique d'évaluation des bibliothèques et centres documentaires*. Paris: Éditions du Cercle de la Librairie, 2001.

Godby, Carol Jean, Smith Devon, Childress, Eric (2003). "Two paths to interoperable metadata." Paper presented at the *2003 Dublin Core Conference, DC-2003: supporting comunities of discourse and practice – metadata research & applications*, September 28-October 2, in Seattle, Washington (USA). Available at: http://www.oclc.org/research/publications/archive/2003/godby-dc2003.pdf

Golub, Koraljka (2006). "Automated subject classification of textual web documents" *Journal of documentation*, v.62 no.3 p.350-371.

González, Wenceslao J. (1997). "Progreso científico e innovación tecnológica: la "tecnociencia" y el problema de las relaciones entre filosofía de la ciencia y filosofía de la tecnología." *Arbor* [Madrid], t. 157, no.620 (Agosto), p. 261-283.

Górny, Mirosław (1994). "Kooperacyjne i bierne formy opracowywania zbiorów bibliotecznych przegląd istniejących rozwiązań w zakresie katalogowania" *Przegląd biblioteczny* nr.1/2 p.97-102.

Górny, Mirosław (2002). "Czas jako ilościowa miara jakości usług bibliotecznych." *Elektroniczny Biuletyn Informacyjny Bibliotekarzy*, Nr 2/2002 (31). Available at: http://ebib.oss.wroc.pl/2002/31/gorny.php

Graham, Peter S. (1990). "Quality in cataloging: making distinctions" *Journal of academic librarianship* v.16 no.4 p.213-218.

Guerrini, Mauro (1999). *Riflessioni su principi, standard, regole e applicazionni: saggi di storia, teoria e tecnica della catalogazione.* Udine: Forum.

Guerrini, Mauro (2002). *Il catalogo di qualità.* Firenze: Pagnini..

Guía (1998). *Guía para la aplicación de la norma ISO 9000 a bibliotecas y servicios de información y documentación.* Madrid: SEDIC.

Harris, Roy (1973). *Synonymy and linguistic analysis.* Oxford: Blackwell; Toronto: University of Toronto.

Harris, Roy (2003). *History, science and the limits of language: an integrationist approach.* Shimla: Indian Institute of Advanced Study.

Harvey, Pierre-Léonard (2002). "La connaissance au-delà du savoir à l'ère des inforoutes: de la diffusion de l'information à la création du sens dans les bibliothèques virtuelles" *Documentation et bibliothèques* v. 48 nr.1 (Jan/Mar) p.5-9.

Heck, André (2001). "Information handling in astronomy: beyond technologies and methodologies" *High energy physics libraries webzine*, issue 3 (March). Available at: http://library.cern.ch/HEPLW/3/papers/2/

Hill, Debra W. (1998). "To outsource or not: University of Alabama libraries engage in pilot project with OCLC's TechPro" *Cataloging and classification quarterly* v.26 nr.1 p.63-73.

Hjørland, Birger (2000). "Vidensorganisation: skal bibliotekarer organisere al information på Internettet?" *Human IT: tidskrift för studier av IT ur ett humanvetenskapligt perspektiv* nr.4, 22 p. Available at: www.hb.se/bhs/ith/4-00/bh.html

Hollnagel, Erik (1993). *Human reliability analysis: context and control.* London: Academic Press.

Hollnagel, Erik (2002). "Dependability of joint human-computer systems." In: S. Anderson et al., eds., *Computer safety, reliability and security: 21st International Conference, SAFECOMP 2002,* Catania, Italy, September 10-13. (Lecture notes in computer science, v.2434) Berlin: Springer, p.4-9.

Hollnagel, Erik; Woods, David D. (2005). *Joint cognitive systems: foundations of cognitive systems engineering.* Boca Raton: CRC.

Innocenti, Piero (1984). "Le pinne del merluzzo e la coda del delfino: qualità e quantità nella procedura di ricerca bibliografica," *Biblioteche oggi,* v.2, nr.4, p. 23-45. Reprinted in Innocenti (1999).

Innocenti, Piero (1999). *Metodi e tecniche nella ricerca bibliografica (trilogia di Mary Poppins).* Manziana (Roma): Vecchiarelli.

Jahier, Stefania; Accarisi, Massimo (2001). "Dialogo sulla qualità: la biblioteca tra programmazione, norme ISO customer satisfaction" In: Foglieni, ed., *La qualità nel sistema biblioteca,* p.231-238.

Jochum, Uwe; Wagner, Gerhard (1998). "Religionsersatz: oder die Vollendung der Gnosis im Internet." In: U. Jochum and G. Wagner, eds., *Am Ende das Buch: semiotische und soziale Aspekte des Internet.* Konstanz: UVK Universitätsverlag, p.139-159.

Kerdellant, Christine (2000). *Le prix de l'incompétence: histoire des grandes erreurs de management.* Paris: Denoël.

Keriguy, Jacques; Dalhoumi, Salah (1991). "Faut-il brûler les bibliothèques? Réflexions à partir d'enquêtes menées dans plusieurs services d'information." In: Liebaers and Walckiers, eds., *Library automation and networking,* p.96-108.

Kocójowa, Maria, ed. (2004). *Przestrzeń informacji i komunikacji społecznej.* Kraków: Wydawnictwo Uniwersytetu Jagiellońskiego.

Kuperman, Aaron Wolfe (2006). Email to David Bade, 28 Sept. 2006.

LaFollette, Marcel C. (2000). "Observations on fraud and scientific integrity in a digital environment" *Journal of the American Society for Information Science* v.51 nr.14 p.1334-1337.

Langer, Ellen J. (1989). "Minding matters: the consequences of mindlessness-mindfulness" *Advances in experimental social psychology* v.22 p.137-173.

Lee, Yang W. (2004). "Crafting rules: context-reflective data quality problem solving" *Journal of management information systems* v.20 no.3 p.93-119.

Lévy-Leblond, Jean-Marc (1996). *Aux contraires: l'exercise de la pensée et la pratique de la science.* Paris: Gallimard.

Liebaers, Herman; Walckiers, Marc, eds. (1991). *Library automation and networking: new tools for a new identity, european conference,* 9-11 may 1990, Brussels = *L'automatisation et les réseaux de bibliothéques : de nouveaux outils pour une identité nouvelle.* Conférence européenne, 9-11 mai 1990, Bruxelles. München: Saur.

Lupovici, Christian (1996). "Les bibliothèques et le défi de l'édition électronique" *Bulletin des bibliothèques de France* t.41 no 1 p.26-31.

Maisonneuve, Marc (1996). "La réalité juridique du traitement des notices bibliographiques. In: M.-E. Freon, ed., *Controler la qualité et la coherence d'un catalogue,* p.35-40.

Mann, Thomas (2005). *Survey of library user studies.* Available at: http://www.guild2910.org/google.htm

Mann, Thomas (2006a). *The changing nature of the catalog and its integration with other discovery tools. Final report. March 17, 2006. Prepared for the Library of Congress by Karen Calhoun. A critical review.* Available at: http://guild2910.org/AFSCMECalhounReviewREV.pdf

Mann, Thomas (2006b). *What is going on at the Library of Congress?* Available at: http://www.guild2910.org

Marcum, Deanna B. (1997). "Digital libraries: For whom? For what?" *Journal of academic librarianship* v.23, March, p.81-84.

Marcum, Deanna B. (2005). "The future of cataloging." *EBSCO Information Services' Executive Seminar at 2005 Midwinter meeting of the America Library Association,* January 16, 2005. Library of Congress, http://www.loc.gov/library/reports/CatalogingSpeech.pdf

Marsh, Stephen; Dibben, Mark R. (2003). "The role of trust in information science and technology" *Annual review of information science and technology* v.37 p.465-498.

Marty, Paul F. (2005). "Factors influencing error recovery in collections databases: a museum case study" *Library Quarterly* v.75 no.3, p.295-328.

Mayère, Anne; Muet, Florence (1998). "La démarche qualité appliquée aux bibliothèques et services d'information: conception et spécificités" *Bulletin des bibliothèques de France* t.43 no.1 p.11-19.

Melot, Michel (1993). "Les nouveaux enjeux de la normalisation" *Bulletin des bibliothèques de France* t.38 no 5 p.10-12.

Morel, Christian (2003). *Les décisions absurdes: sociologie des erreurs radicales et persistantes.* Paris: nrf Gallimard.

"Mort et transfiguration des catalogues." *Bulletin des bibliothèques de France*, t. 50 nr.4, 2005.

Naumann, Felix (2001). "From databases to information systems: information quality makes the difference." In: *Proceedings of the International Conference on Information Quality*, 2001, MIT. Available at: http://www.hqiq.de/publications.html

Naumann, Felix (2002). *Quality-driven query answering for integrated information systems.* (Lecture notes in computer science, 2261) Berlin: Springer.

Naumann, Felix; Rolker, Claudia (1999). "Do metadata models meet IQ requirements?" In: *Proceedings of the International Conference on Information Quality 1999 (IQ'99)*, MIT. Available at: http://hqiq.de/publications.html

Nehmy, Rosa Maria Quadros; Paim, Isis (1998). "A desconstrução do conceito de "qualidade da informação." *Ciência da informação*, v.27 n.1 (Jan.-Apr.) p.36-45.

Nord, G. Daryl; Nord, Jeretta Horn; Xu, Hongjiang (2005). "An investigation of the impact of organization size on data quality issues" *Journal of database management* v.16 no.3 p.58-71.

Oberhauser, Otto (2005). "Automatisches Klassifizieren und Bibliothekskataloge." In: H. Hrusa, ed., *Bibliothek Technik Recht: Festschrift für Peter Kubalek zum 60. Geburtstag*. Wien: Manz. p.119-131. Available at: http://eprints.rclis.org/archive/00004833/

Oddy, Pat (1999). "The case for international co-operation in cataloguing: from copy cataloguing to multilingual subject access — experiences within the British Library" *Program* v.33 no.1 (January), p.29-39.

Orlikowski, Wanda J. (1991). "Integrated information environment or matrix of control? The contradictory implications of information technology" *Accounting, management and information technology* v.1 no.1 p.9-42.

Orlikowski, Wanda J.; Barley, Stephen R. (2001). "Technology and institutions: what can research on information technology and research on organizations learn from each other?" *MIS quarterly* v.25 no.2 (June) p.145-165.

Orlikowski, Wanda J.; Iacono, C. Suzanne (2001). "Research commentary: Desperately seeking the "IT" in IT research—a call to theorizing the IT artifact" *Information systems research* v.12, no.2 (June), p.121-134.

Ørsted, Jeannette (2001). "Quality and efficiency: incompatible elements in translation practice?" *Meta: journal des traducteurs* v.46, nr.2 p.438-447.

Paim, Isis; Nehmy, Rosa Maria Quadros; Guimarães, César Geraldo (1996). "Problematização do conceito "Qualidade" da informação." *Perspectivas em ciência da informação*, v.1 n.1 (Jan.-Jun.) p.111-119.

Parasuraman, Raja; Riley, Victor (1997). "Humans and automation: use, misuse, disuse, abuse" *Human factors* v.39, nr.2, p.230-253.

Park, Jung-ran (2006). "Semantic interoperability and metadata quality: an analysis of metadata item records of digital image collections." *Knowledge organization* v.33 no.1 p.20-34.

Patrick, Robert L.; Black, Donald V. (1964). "Index files: their loading and organization for use." In: B.E. Markuson, ed., *Libraries and automation: Proceedings of the Conference on Libraries and Automation held at Airlie Foundation*, Warrenton, Virginia, May 26-30, 1963. Washington, D.C.: Library of Congress, p.29-48.

Perrow, Charles (1984). *Normal accidents: living with high-risk technologies.* New York: Basic Books.

Pew, Gordon (2007). Re: [ACAT] *Qualifying headings.* Posting to Autocat, 31 August 2007.

Pinto Molina, Maria (1998). "Gestión de calidad en documentación" *Anales de documentación,* v.1 p.171-183. Available at: http://eprints.rclis.org/archive/00002726

Pogányné Rózsa Gabriella (1999). "'A címleíró [...] munkája rossz lesz, ha csak a szabályt tartja szem előtt s nem egyúttal az embert is, kinek számára a címeket leírja.' Domanovszky Ákos emlékezete," *Könyv, könyvtár, könyvtáros,* Dec. 1999, p.50-54.

Poyet, Christine (1990). "L'homme, agent de fiabilité dans les systèmes automatisés." In: Leplat and Terssac, eds., *Les facteurs humains de la fiabilité dans les systèmes complexes,* p.223-240.

Preece, Barbara G.; Fox, Mary Anne (1992). "Preliminary LC records for monographs in OCLC" *Information technology and libraries* v.11 March, p.3-9.

Rasmussen, Jens; Duncan, Keith; and Leplat, Jacques, eds. (1987). *New technology and human error.* Chichester: John Wiley & Sons.

Reason, James (1995). "A systems approach to organizational error" *Ergonomics* v.38 no.8 p.1708-1721.

Revelli, Carlo (2004). "La mattanza dei catalogatori: una funzione che rischia la dequalificazione" *Biblioteche oggi,* June 2004, p.7-15.

Rickover, Hyman G. (1979). "Management in government" *Management* (September 1979, p.16-19.

Rickover, Hyman G. (1982). "Doing a job" (Speech delivered at Columbia University in 1982). Excerpt available at: http://www.govleaders.org/rickover.htm

Robertson, R. John; Barton, Jane (2005). "Optimising metadata workflows in a distributed information environment." In: *9th DELOS thematic workshop—Digital Repositories: Interoperability and Common Services*, 11-13 May, 2005, Crete. pp. 1-8. Available at: http://eprints.rclis.org/archive/00005995/

Rochlin, Gene I., La Porte, Todd R.; Roberts, Karlene H. (1987). "The self-designing high-reliability organization: aircraft carrier flight operations at sea" *Naval War College review.* Autumn, p.76–90; repr. Summer 1998, p.97–113. Available at: www.nwc.navy.mil/press/Review/1998/summer/art7su98.htm

Ruiz Quintanilla, S. Antonio (1987). "New technologies and human error: social and organizational factors." In: Rasmussen et al. *New technology and human error,* p. 125-128.

Santarsiero, Marisa (2001). "La gestione per la qualità: dal budget all'offerta dei servizi" In: Franz Berger and Klaus Kempf, eds., *Riforma universitaria e rivoluzione dei media,* p.75-83.

Sapori, Giuliana (1995). "La qualità del catalogo come presupposto di una efficace ricerca bibliografica." In: Anna Maria Cozzi and Ornella Foglieni, eds., *L'automazione delle biblioteche delle università: l'esperienza della base SBN delle università degli studi di Milano* il 26 e 27 ottobre 1992. Milano: Regione Lombardia, p.59-64.

Sawyer, Jeanne C.; Davis, Jinnie Y. (1984). "Automated error detection in library systems." In: M. Gorman, ed., *Crossroads: proceedings of the First National Conference of the Library and Information Technology Association,* September 17-1, 1983, Baltimore, Maryland. Chicago: ALA, p.213-217.

Skipper, James E. (1967). "International implications of the Shared Cataloging Program: introductory statement" *Libri* v.17 nr.4 p.270-275.

Sotto, Richard (1990). *Man without knowledge: actors and spectators in organizations.* Stockholm: Företagsekonomiska institutionen Stockholms universitet.

Stankowski, R.R.H. (1990). "Bibliographic record maintenance and control in a consortium database" *Cataloging & classification quarterly* v.12 nr2 p.47-62.

Stokić (2004). Стокић, Гордана. "Библиотеке и управљање укупним квалитетом" *Глас библиотеке* nr.11 p. 41-50. Available at: http://eprints.rclis.org/archive/00003928/

Svagelski-Liassine, F. (1990). "Erreur." In: S. Auroux, ed., *Encyclopédie philosophique universelle. II: Les notions philosophiques: dictionaire*, t. 1, p. 833-835.

Svenonius, Elaine (2000). *The intellectual foundation of information organization*. Cambridge: MIT Press.

Thibault, Brigitte; Freon, Marie-Elise (1996). "Definir des objectifs de qualité en tenant compte des differentes bibliothèques." In: M.-E. Freon, ed., *Controler la qualité et la coherence d'un catalogue*, p.25-32.

Thomas, Sarah E. (1996). "Quality in bibliographic control" *Library trends* Winter 1996, v.44 nr.3 p.491-505.

Thomas, Sarah E.(2000). *The catalog as portal to the Internet*. Available at: http://www.loc.gov/catdir/bibcontrol/thomas_paper.html.

Truitt, Marc (2006). "On 'earth-shaking matters'..." Available in the Autocat archives for 30 August 2006.

University of California Libraries. Bibliographic Services Task Force (2005). *Rethinking how we provide bibliographic services for the University of California*. Available at: http://libraries.universityofcalifornia.edu/sopag/BSTF/Final.pdf

University of Chicago, Provost's Task Force on the University Library (2006). *Final report*. Available at: http://www.lib.uchicago.edu/staffweb/groups/space/finalreport.html

Valdés Abreu, Manuela de la Caridad (2001). "Consideraciones generales en torno al valor añadido de la información" *Biblios* v.8. Originally published: *ACIMED* 1999, v.7 nr.1. Available at: http://eprints.rclis.org/archive/00002462/

Valles, Miguel S. (2005). "El reto de la calidad en la investigación social cualitativa: de la retórica a los planteamientos de fondo y las propuestas técnicas." *Reis (Revista española de investigaciones sociológicas)* v.110 (Abril-Junio 2005) p.91-114.

Van Fraassen, Bas C. (2004). "Science as representation: flouting the criteria" Philosophy of science v.71 nr.5 (*PSA 2002: proceedings of the 2002 biennial meeting of the Philosophy of Science Association. Part II, Symposia papers*), p.794-804.

Večerník, Jiří; Hvížďala, Karel (2003). "O rychlosti, kvalitě a ceně informací." In: K. Hvížďala, *Moc a nemoc médií: rozhovory, eseje a články 2000-2003*. Praha: Máj; Dokořán, p.45-49.

Vestrucci, Paolo (1990). *Modelli per la valutazione dell'affidabilità umana.* Milano: Franco Angeli.

Wand, Yair; Wang, Richard Y. (1996). "Anchoring data quality dimensions in ontological foundations" *Communications of the ACM* v.39 no.11 (Nov.) p.86-95.

Weick, Karl E. (1987). "Organizational culture as a source of high reliability" *California management review* v.29 nr.2 p.112-127.

Weick, Karl E.; Sutcliffe, Kathleen M. (2001). *Managing the unexpected: assuring high performance in an age of complexity.* San Francisco: Jossey-Bass.

Weick, Karl E.; Sutcliffe, Kathleen M.; Obstfeld, David (1999). "Organizing for high reliability: processes of collective mindfulness" *Research in organizational behavior* v.21 p.81-123.

Weisberg, Michael (2004). "Qualitative theory and chemical explanation" *Philosophy of science* v.71 nr.5 (PSA 2002: proceedings of the 2002 biennial meeting of the Philosophy of Science Association. Part II, Symposia papers), p.1071-1081.

Wiener, Norbert (1956). *The human use of human beings.* 2nd ed., rev. New York: Doubleday Anchor.

Witt, Maria (1993). "La normalisation et le bibliothécaire" *Bulletin des bibliothèques de France*, t. 38, no 5 p.37-39.

Wojciechowski, Jacek (2004). "Biblioteczne rekomendacje i filtracje." In: Kocójowa, ed., *Przestrzeń informacji i komunikacji społecznej*, p.248-255.

Wood, Geoffrey; Frynas, Jędrzej George (2006). "The institutional basis of economic failure: anatomy of the segmented business system" *Socio-economic review* 4, p.239-277.

Woods, David D.; Hollnagel, Erik (2006). *Joint cognitive systems: patterns in cognitive systems engineering.* Boca Raton: CRC Press.

Wormell, Irene, ed. (1990). *Information quality: definitions and dimensions: proceedings of a NORDINFO seminar, Royal School of Librarianship*, Copenhagen, 1989. London: Taylor Graham.

Woźniak, Jadwiga (2002). "Mój OPAC świadczy o mnie, czyli krótko o ważniejszych aspektach oceny jakości komputeriowych katalogów bibliotecznych." *Biuletyn biblioteki Jagiellońskiej* r.52 p.17-23.

Yang, Chyan; Yang, Keng-Chieh; and Yuan Hsu-Chieh (2007). "Improving the search process through ontology-based adaptive semantic search" *The Electronic library* v.25 no.2 p.234-248.

Zybert, Elżbieta Barbara (2004). "Kultura jakości – przyszłością bibliotek." In: M. Kocójowa, ed., *Przestrzeń informacji i komunikacji społecznej*, p.256-266.

Letter to Autocat concerning LC's Series Treatment Decision, May 31, 2006

Dear friends:

The recent announcement of LC's decision concerning series authority records has given rise to considerable discussion about a number of issues which have concerned me for many years. The comments which I wish to make are, like many recent posts, intended to relate this single issue (series authorities decisions at one library) to more fundamental issues that involve us all. These are: 1) nature of cooperation and resource sharing; 2) successful bibliographic (re)search; 3) purpose and goals of cataloging; 4) direction and manner of change.

1) Cooperation. It is a fundamental principle of cooperation that all parties involved do their share of the work A cooperative agreement in which one partner (e.g. LC) or a few is/are expected to do all or most of the work succeeds only so long as those partners continue doing the work in a satisfactory manner. The decision to cease providing series records is simply the latest evidence that the success of our cooperative agreements depends upon the reliability of the cooperating institutions. The decisions of OCLC to allow vendor records and Cornell's below minimal level records should have sparked an even stronger opposition. Since most libraries have assumed the contributions of LC and all others, staff have been reduced to minimum (or lower) and now there is simply no possibility of picking up the extra work load. Predictions concerning shared cataloging led many libraries for many years to eliminate or not fill cataloger positions in the expectation that our cataloging will be done by someone at another institution. I think that everyone knows at this point that some (how many?) PCC libraries will follow LC regardless of the official PCC stance because they have no adequate staff to take up what LC formerly did. LC knows this too.

In order for cooperation to work for all involved, the nature, purpose and goals of the work must be clearly understood and affirmed by all participants. These have been clearly stated in a number of public policy documents and it is toward the satisfaction of these publicly stated professional goals that most catalogers orient their work. Yet in a shared database such as OCLC the enormous diversity of participating institutions creates problems for determining mutually acceptable goals. Vendors need order records, not research tools. Public libraries cater to a user community which differs markedly from the academic users of a research library. Rare books require a significantly greater attention to description than current academic monographs, for which subject analysis is more important. Some members of the profession have an overriding concern with user perceptions of the ease of searching (everything through a single box Google style) and are satisfied with "getting information"; the model of the user for these librarians is the high school or undergraduate student who is required to "include a bibliography of at least 5 sources excluding encyclopedias." Others more concerned with the thorough and intelligent searching which serious scholarship requires argue for detailed subject indexing of all materials which alone will support cross-language subject searching. In a database created and maintained by participants with so many conflicting understandings of the goals of the information created and entered into the database, these local and conflicting goals must be pursued locally, which of course requires local staff.

In a cooperative database serving such disparate institutional needs, the option for local control of local demands depends upon local staffing; where staff are too few in number or lacking the requisite range of skills, the only options are either following whatever everybody else does or the abandonment of any evaluation for locally appropriate and adequate information.

2) Research. I use Google. A lot. But Ms. Marcum's insistence on the sufficiency of and preference of researchers for Google over the library catalog is tellingly illustrated with an account of how an undergraduate now goes about writing a paper, even stressing that the student wants an A. (http://www.loc.gov/library/reports/CatalogingSpeech.pdf) Ms. Calhoun's report to LC was based on a review of a small portion of the last 5 years work in the English language. To do research as described by Marcum or published by Calhoun one does not need a library and certainly not a librarian, whether cataloger or administrator. Nor does one need a library catalog. However, some of us younger folk make much more rigorous demands of scholarship, not only of the argumentation but for the literature search as well. *If* everything were free and available with fulltext

online, then *perhaps* neither a library nor a librarian would be necessary. But everything is not online and we must live in the actual present rather than in someone's plans and dreams for the future. In the actual present most of the worlds' published material is not available online anywhere, and much of what is online is only available to subscribers. In this situation, which is ours, we need to be able to find what is available to us here and now in the library to which we have access. And when we find citations anywhere, through whatever means to relevant material which is not available online, we need to be able to find out whether or not it is available in or through our library and if so where and how to obtain it. We can, of course, digitize everything we have (necessitating many copyright violations) or at least our bibliographical information and make it available for web search engines to index, thereby allowing or even forcing everyone to use Google to find out what is in the library. Yet if we do the latter—contribute bibliographic information—then someone has to do that in some intelligible and searchable manner. If one wants to search by author, the author has to be identified as an author—rather than the title—and the same goes for series searching and every other kind of specific (intelligent) searching.

The trouble with Marcum, Calhoun et al. is that they are arguing for information seeking rather than research, and in this model, any information found implies a successful search. The Google model of information seeking is not a model of intelligent research; it is a model of easy information gathering. For someone who wants "a bibliography," Google works. For someone who wants "the bibliography," Google searching is a wonderful starting point and a great last minute source for recent materials, but if Google alone is used, it fails miserably. No matter what the subject, one need only compare what a Google search retrieves with what one can find in a good multilingual bibliography on your topic to realize the extent of Google's failure as a one-stop research method. Rather than taking a survey to determine what "most people" do first or last or find easiest, professional librarians in academic institutions ought to be responsible for developing, implementing and *teaching* a variety of methods, each of which may be appropriate for several different types of search/research but not necessarily useful or adequate for others.

3) Cataloging. The simplest argument for the continued necessity of cataloging is the demand for cataloging born-digital materials

available online. The next simplest argument is that there is no machine of any sort which can take a book, article, painting, piece of music or computer file and inform the searcher of the book's (computer file's, score's, etc.) title, author, publisher, etc. Either these kinds of information about every document must be entered into the machine in a machine-readable fashion by someone who can interpret the document, or every item must be so standardized that the interpretation of the particular significance of every bit of text (sound, color, etc.) follows from its location in the item. The vast numbers of hits in a Google search is due to the fact that everything has the same significance in a Google search: one cannot search for authors, composers, titles, publishers etc. in any other way than as bits of text of no particular significance. Thus a Google search for Mongol and Java retrieves 326,000 hits, while a search for Mongols and Java retrieves 116,000. In contrast, a search in OCLC provides 10 hits, 9 of which are of very limited interest or useless (e.g. maps of the Mongol empire and general books on the Mongols), while a search in the Regenstein Library catalog retrieves 2 books, the only two non-fictional books ever written on the topic of the Mongol invasion of Jawa, neither of which are available online, both of which have multilingual bibliographies. Furthermore, only the more recently published book appears in the OCLC search due to the poor subject analysis provided for the earlier book.

Information technologies are helpless without information, and worthless if misinformation is input. The Indiana University white paper *The Future of Cataloging* recognizes this while the Calhoun report does not. One of the chief defects of automated indexing and analysis is the high rate of production of misinformation. In this respect, I have found that automatic indexing produces records similar in quality to the below minimal records produced by Cornell: very bad to totally useless. David Banush of Cornell has so lovingly suggested in a posting to PCCPOL list that catalogers are an aging and conservative group of secure and comfortable bureaucrats "vigorously (sometimes stridently) defending the status quo, or even the status quo ante" whose "prospects for long-term growth in a very dynamic global information economy are dim." I would reply that the prospects for long-term growth of an information economy without high quality information are even dimmer.

The library and the information economy in which it is embedded is portrayed in Marcum's papers, the Calhoun report, the California report and even the Indiana University white paper as a technical system in which there is no hint of the possibility of error and misinformation and how that will effect the efficiency of the technical system itself. There is a desperate need for library administrators to read in depth the ergonomic literature on error and that on failure in organizations. (I recommend Bogner *Human error in medicine*, Dörner, *The logic of failure*, Hoc et al., *Expertise and technology*, Hollnagel *Cognitive reliability and error analysis method*, Hollnagel and Woods, *Joint cognitive systems*, Kerdellant *Le prix de l'incompétence*, Lagadec *La civilisation du risque*, Leplat and Terssac (eds.) *Les facteurs humains de la fiabilité dans les systèmes complexes*, Merry and Smith, *Errors, medicine and the law*, Morel, *Les décisions absurdes*, Reason *Human error*, Silverman *Critiquing human error*, Rasmussen et al. *New technology and human error*, Vestrucci *Modelli per la valutazione dell'affidabilità umana*, Woods et al., *Behind human error*, Frese and Zapf (eds.), *Fehler bei der Arbeit mit dem Computer*, and all of the writings on high reliability organizations of Karl Weick. I have dealt with these matters at length in *Theory and practice of bibliographic failure*, and in a recent paper of mine I looked at the library catalog as a communication system, combining linguistic aspects of information retrieval and human error research: "Colorless green ideals in the language of bibliographic description," *Language & Communication* 2007, v.27:1 p.54-80.)

4) Change. Perhaps the most disastrous and shortsighted aspect of policy decisions such as minimal level records and the abandonment of series authorities is the fact that future technological capabilities will depend—as they do now—on the presence rather than the absence of information in the record. As many commentators have remarked, automatic authority checking both for correction of mistakes and for collocation in the presence of variation ONLY works if the information is both transcribed from the piece into the bibliographical record and the correct / authorized / standard form established in an authority file. Without that double aspect of bibliographic description and control no automatic error correction and no collocation software presently available or in the future will ever be possible. On these matters library administrators are almost universally technologically ignorant and have absolutely no idea how information technologies work and what are the minimum requirements for their successful implementation. Almost every change demanded by the Karen Calhouns

and Deanna Marcums will ensure failure in the implementation of any future technological developments.

Summary:

- There are vast differences in the expectations of the various users for what the shared utilities should accept and provide (book vendors vs. PCC Full Level standards).

- There are at least 2 completely different and mutually exclusive understandings of what research is and what researchers require (Calhoun vs. T. Mann).

- There are those who believe that information technologies do not require structured information or that software and/or the market will provide whatever is needed efficiently and adequately for research needs, and there are others who believe that information technologies are marvelous tools which require intelligent input and use, and that given the needs of academic research, the necessary production of information for technological manipulation and exploitation can only be successfully accomplished by persons who share the intellectual backgrounds, commitments and research activities of the academic community.

- There are those who believe that current promises of future technological possibilities must be believed and no alternative futures may be considered, and there are those who, cognizant of the preceding three professional debates and dilemmas surrounding cooperation, research practices and data quality, would reject all institutional action and forecasting that has been narrowly determined by technological hopes and expectations.

Sincerely,

David Bade
Joseph Regenstein Library
University of Chicago

Structures, standards, and the people who make them meaningful

A good way to begin any discussion of bibliographical control is to remember Ashby's *Law of Requisite Variety*. A simple version of this is

> (1) The amount of appropriate selection that can be performed is limited by the amount of information available. (2) For appropriate regulation the variety in the regulator must be equal to or greater than the variety in the system being regulated.[1]

I would prefer to draw out the implications of that for our work, but we have been asked to respond to a set of questions (for those questions, see Fallgren, 2007c). The questions to which we were asked to respond, like these meetings themselves, rest upon certain assumptions that I want to note and comment upon before I make any response to the particulars. The chief difficulties I had with the background paper had to do with the understanding of what goes on in libraries, why, and for whom. Additionally, the ways in which we understand users, policies and technologies and the relationships among these elements are crucial determinants for how we think about structures and standards. To start with, then, let me note three assumptions from the background paper:

1) There are two main users of bibliographic data and their associated use environments: consumers and management.
2) Structures and standards govern the creation, recording, and distribution of metadata in bibliographic control
3) Data are created to be processed by applications.

---

[1] "Law of Requisite Variety", in *Web Dictionary of Cybernetics and Systems* http://pespmc1.vub.ac.be/ASC/LAW_VARIE.html (viewed 8 May 2007). The more technical formulation as it appears in Ashby's *Introduction to Cybernetics* (1956: p. 207) is: V_D is given and fixed, $V_D - V_R$ can be lessened only by a corresponding increase in V_R. Thus the variety in the outcomes, if minimal, can be decreased further only by a corresponding increase in that of R. (A more general statement is given in S.11/9.) This is the law of Requisite Variety. To put it more picturesquely: only variety in R can force down the variety due to D; variety can destroy variety.

The first two assumptions are reflected in the first question: What kinds of structures and standards are needed to provide effective bibliographic control in the environmental spectrum spanning consumer uses and management uses? The variety of users and user purposes so noticeable in the background paper for the first meeting disappeared in the reports of that meeting and the second background paper. The third assumption indicates that the paper rests upon an understanding of what happens in libraries that is rooted in a theory of transportation rather than a theory of communication. The background paper in general assumes that what happens in libraries can be described as a technical system, not a communication system. In this model data are not created for people but for processing by applications. Supply chains, repositories, database silos, data flows, mining, manipulation and display: this is the language of the background paper, and it is not the language of communication. My understanding of structures and standards is rooted in a very different view of what happens in libraries. So let me reorient the discussion of structures and standards, and bibliographic control in general, according to my understanding that what happens in libraries is communication, not transportation.

The philosopher H.P. Grice offered nine maxims as the general standards governing communication:

1. Make your contribution as informative as is required
2. Do not make your contribution more informative than is required
3. Do not say what you believe to be false
4. Do not say that for which you lack adequate evidence
5. Be relevant
6. Avoid obscurity of expression
7. Avoid ambiguity
8. Be brief
9. Be orderly

Grice noted that communicative exchanges are characteristically cooperative efforts in which participants recognize a common purpose or orientation. He offered a single principle—the co-operative principle—which he suggested must inform communicative activity: Make your conversation contribution such as is required, at the stage at which it occurs, by the accepted purpose of direction of the talk exchange in which you are engaged.²

So first of all, three things to note: communication, cooperation and common purposes. Beyond these critical matters, we notice that these standards would please most library administrators AND all users, including catalogers, reference librarians, and acquisitions personnel. Another thing that we should notice is that these standards are not the same kinds of standards as ISBD which only describes how one presents certain information. These Gricean standards are not just about how but about what information should be put forth.

The order in which I will proceed is as follows: first remarks on structures and standards for facilitating communication, then a discussion of users and uses followed by comments on cooperation and the conflicting goals that this inevitably involves. Comments on understanding technologies, in particular metadata harvesting and datamining lead into a set of more specific observations as responses to the questions.

Structures and standards to facilitate communication, not data transport

The first task then is to understand libraries as communication systems. Grice's standards are standards for communication between and among human beings. In contrast, the theory of librarianship which informed the background paper is unmistakably a theory of industrial production, transportation and storage, in which meaning is "mined" rather than created, and information flows and is merged and manipulated *but never interpreted, evaluated or corrected*. The failure to even mention these activities is a glaring—and revealing—omission in the Working Group's statements and questions asked of the speakers at these meetings.

If bibliographical information is created in an attempt to communicate to someone, then the relationship between that someone and the creators of that information is the locus of meaning in libraries—not the structures, standards and technologies used in that communicative activity. The possibilities for the success or failure of that communication are rooted in the indeterminacy of predicting what, why and how those for whom the information is created will be searching.

---

² Grice (1975), p.45-46.

What can be done is to fashion the information created according to those social practices that both the library user and the library expect in each particular institution. Those practices are both fashioned by and revealed in the publications being cataloged themselves: forms of citation, tables of contents, indexing terms, abstracts, statements of authorship, readership or sponsorship, links, theoretical orientation, timeliness, genre and the like.

In addition to knowing the social practices served by the institution, another key factor for successful communication is that the person creating the bibliographical information must actually have something to communicate. Communication is successful when the hearer can infer the speaker's meaning, Sperber and Wilson maintained.[3] A cataloger or reference librarian who cannot read and understand the items of interest is of no more use than a machine that cannot, and sometimes probably worth less. Incomprehension of the language of the text or of the discipline makes communication impossible. The impossibility of communication in any situation of incomprehension has clear implications for all efforts to automate the creation of bibliographical information.

Moving to the more specific matters at hand, communication requires a medium and it is characteristic of all means of communication that they have differing potentials and limitations, and that they are socially regulated. There is a certain range of physical requirements and capacities associated with signing, speaking, writing and online searching with a mouse. It is equally true that all of these practices are neither innate nor intuitive but learned and socially regulated. This is just as true of Flickr as it is of LCSH, of "natural language" as it is of scientific terminology. Different persons combine and use different means of communication according to their situation and purposes to further their communicational goals. This leads us to the second matter, the subject of the first meeting: users.

Users and uses

Karen Coyle noted on her blog the inadequacies of the dichotomous model of users identified in the first meeting of the Working

---

[3] Sperber and Wilson (1986), p.23. I would prefer to say "when the hearer can respond appropriately to the speaker's meaning."

Group.[4] Consumers and managers are the two user models the paper offers, and the first set of questions we have been asked to respond to follows from that identification. Unless the multiple user groups and their widely varying uses are clearly articulated, how can anyone possibly respond to the first question? The goals of management can often be achieved simply by attaching a number to a book and also to a computer record. Mark it and park it: every cataloger has heard this from an administrator. Nothing else is needed to move a book from acquisitions through binding and labeling to storage, into the hands of the patron and back again. For the student who merely wants something quick Google suffices and the library need only have Internet access; students often want nothing more, even when they could benefit from more. For the historian of 13th century Jawa—not a fictional user, but me—a vast array of bibliographic tools of all sorts are needed to effectively cover literature in dozens of languages spanning 700 years.

The division between consumers and managers has certain implications. The most important implication is that consuming and managing presuppose the prior existence of information. What is left out of this dichotomy is the creation of information: who is doing that? The consumers or the managers? The answer of course is neither of these, but a third category of shadowy characters largely left out of account in the background paper's understanding of what happens in libraries. Many years ago Jean-Pierre Dupuy insisted that only if you ignore the creation of information and the meaning of information can you treat it as a thing in a technical process.[5] This is precisely what we find in the background paper.

If consumers and managers are to consume and manage information, then someone has to create it, and in that act we can locate the essential task of the library: to provide the library's users with information about what the library has to offer. And it is precisely in this context—the individual organization, whether that is the University of Chicago, OCLC or Google Book Search—that bibliographical control is meaningful and necessary. That may mean searching other information sources for information to use for one's own purposes, but in every case that information is not simply a repetition or copying of existing information. Putting that information from whatever source

---

[4] Coyle (2007c)
[5] Dupuy (1980).

into the local database is the creation of new information about location and availability, assertions of propriety and relevance, judgements about value and utility for local users. It is often also an implicit statement of approval (e.g. approval plans), of verified accuracy, and in the better libraries involves the adaptation and increase of bibliographic information with a specific institutional purpose and user community in mind.

The background paper notes that some information can serve both consumers and managers, but that most speakers at the first meeting felt that current bibliographical information and the means of accessing it were inadequate to their needs. Structures and standards do not, however, create bibliographic information: people do. The key issue facing librarians, a matter discernable in the consumer-manager dichotomy, is that of the creation of information: *there is no information, no meaning "out there" to be found, managed, mined, merged, manipulated or processed unless it has been created by someone for some purpose in a form which that creator deemed adequate for the intended users and uses.*

Cooperation and conflicting goals

Many types of libraries exist, serving users with vastly different goals and purposes. When we broaden our view of the bibliographic universe to include book sellers, publishers, commercial databases and other information services, the disparity of goals and purposes are more clearly seen. In cooperative databases and in any situation of autonomous data sources the highest common denominator approaches zero. The information found may not have been created for purposes consonant with one's own institutional goals, and may even make it unsuitable for the library's purposes This leads to the final question from the Background paper:

5. Libraries now manage different flows of data, created within different regimes, much of it outside the library environment. They also want their data and services to appear in other environments. At the same time, we see more reuse and flow of data across publishers, libraries, agents, other bibliographic services, etc. What does this mean for our bibliographic structures and standards?

The use of data created outside the library requires the library to evaluate its appropriateness and adapt it as necessary to the institution's goals, the only other option being to ignore the specific nature of one's own institution along with the corresponding user needs. In a collaborative environment such as OCLC, everything matters to someone so everything ought to matter to every one. The most demanding uses of the most demand-ing users should determine the kind of structures and standards required. The reverse, however, is the case: because of different goals and purposes in the creation of bibliographic information, there is not a single bit of information which matters to everyone. *This is why the primary problem of information from external sources is that nothing can be assumed to be present, correct or adequate.* In other words, the problem of bibliographic control lies within each institution and is determined by its particular purposes and needs.

In the literatures of cognitive psychology, ergonomics and management a significant etiology of failure, disasters and accidents is associated with failures to articulate goals, the articulation of general or vague goals which cover a multitude of disparate and often incompatible goals, and proceeding in a manner which contradicts the stated goals. The successful use of bibliographic information generated outside the institution will always require evaluation and adaptation, and often correction in light of the particular library's goals. So we can say that

No organization can assume that anyone else is committed to serving its users and therefore each organization will have to ensure that all bibliographical information obtained from all sources be evaluated for its users.

Misunderstanding technology

When a technical system is seen as a purely technical system, it is misunderstood. A simplistic view of technology understands the functional efficacy of its objects without grasping the system of interrelations which they create. (Gras, 1993) Hélène Denis (2005, p.78) observed that *[It is] cooperation between professionals that defines the technologies and their reliability, these being not any preexisting reality but a provisional achievement.*

If there is only one thing that you remember from my talk, I hope it is that statement, so let me repeat it: [It is] cooperation between professionals that defines the technologies and their reliability, these being not any preexisting reality but a provisional achievement.

Mechanical creation, mining, harvesting, and interpretation of bibliographic data are often presented as though what these techniques make technically possible is the same thing as what is realizable, that they are neither effected by implementation nor affect the system in which they are implemented. Nothing could be further from the truth. Donald Norman (1990, p.4) observed that "The behavior of an information processing system is not a product of the design specifications; it is a product of the interaction between the human and the system." While technologies understand nothing and have nothing to communicate, human beings can use a wide variety of technologies in their efforts to communicate. In order to understand how that technologically mediated communication among human beings happens, we must understand what technologies actually do, and not be confused by the misleading metaphors which abound in LIS.

Automated methods for description, indexing, subject analysis, classification and relevance ranking all share certain common features: they are based on definitions, axioms, heuristics and the statistical analysis of texts. This means they have no access to the practices and understandings of either the author of the text or the library user who might be looking for that item, with or without knowing it. Statistical statements—about meaning or anything else—are valid only over sufficiently large populations. In the face of the particular, in this unique context, statistical laws are inapplicable and statistical statements have no validity. This means nothing less than that in the automated creation of bibliographic information every bit of information created has only a certain probability of being correct. This requires the following rule for practice:

Quality assessment requires an assessment of the individual records and all machine-generated information must be evaluated by a human being capable of evaluating the results and correcting them if necessary.

To leave evaluation and correction as matters to be attended to only if someone happens to notice is to operate according to what Dörner (1997) called "a repair shop policy," this being one of the most common etiologies of disaster in the management situations which he studied.

What about metadata harvesting and data-mining?

If we look at the move from one-at-a-time cataloging to batch processing, we can see the key issue clearly: if content is a given, produced and obtained from external sources— not produced in and by the institution—then the quality of that content is the responsibility of the producers/providers, not the library. When it is assumed that the required information already exists or will be created elsewhere later, the quality, value and responsibility for the information is located externally. Nauman and Rolker (1999) argued that since "The main source for believability is the author or creator of the information," identifying the creators of information is important for judging information quality. When information is acquired from external sources, determining the reliability of the source is critical, but they note that this cannot be done automatically, and that one must assume that information sources will be very resourceful trying to find ways to improve believability without improving the correctness of the information itself. The matter of authority and provenance you recall was also a significant issue identified by Prof. Burke at the first meeting of the Working Group.

When the work performed in the library is by policy not to be concerned with any issues of quality, complete trust has been placed in the technical system and all sources from which information may be acquired at any point in the process. The result is that the library no longer has any possibility of maintaining a mindful awareness of what is happening and loses the internal variety required to deal with the complexity of the system in its entirety. The policies and organizational structures that I have examined in my research all involve a lapse in reliability, the removal of thought, judgement and responsibility from the persons creating, manipulating and maintaining the database, and hence from the library as a whole. Marsh and Dibben remarked:

> If we are told something in an electronic world, how can we trust it? Previously, a document's credibility was to some extent maintained by knowledge workers such as librarians, editors, and other intermediaries. Today, this front line of information authentification is not always in place. The problem is compounded when one considers that searching for information may be done not by humans but by automated agents. (Marsh and Dibben, 2003, p.484-485)

Trusting external sources of metadata assumes that the ends for which those sources create information are compatible with the particular institution's intended uses of that metadata. For instance booksellers describe books in order to sell them, but what serves the bookseller's purposes may cause serious problems for the bibliographer, reference librarian and library users of all sorts. The first example in the handout should sufficiently illustrate the problem.

Compare the "metadata" in the record with what appears in the book received as fulfillment of an order placed using that order record: The language of the book is French for the entries with Albanian definitions, but the metadata supplied states that the language is Russian. The book is a dictionary but this is not noted in the contents field nor in the subject fields. The title on the book is only in Albanian, but that title is misspelled in the record, and an additional English title not on the book is given. The author given has only a first initial—an incorrect one—while the second author is not given. The place of publication is given as Russia in the fixed fields and misspelled as Tirana in the imprint field. The book has a copyright date of 2004, but in the record the date is given as unknown in the fixed fields and 2000? in the imprint. The pagination is also wrong in the record.

The vendor's metadata and the vendor's book received on that order ought to match, yet the only fields in the entire record which are both present and correct are the ISBN and the publisher's name. Every other field/subfield is either missing, contains errors or is completely wrong. For the bibliographer, cataloger, researcher who has a citation to the actual book, it may well appear that the item described by the bookseller is a different edition, and if searched by author or qualified by date or language, it will not be found at all. The cataloger and the acquisition librarian alike are forced to ask an unanswerable question: did we in fact receive what we ordered or something different?

We can see the same kind of nonsense and inappropriate data everywhere in OCLC in records supplied by libraries, booksellers and cataloging vendors. Glenn Patton wrote to me last year "The basic issue is that we cannot index data that is not there." He was referring to vernacular searching which is only available if vernacular script is entered into the record. Records without subject data in subject fields cannot be retrieved on any subject search. The same goes for every searchable element in a bibliographic record. That missing data is a massive problem in records with transliteration, in recon records, in booksellers' records and in records input by university libraries according to policies for data mining rather than communicating with users. The use of such records in libraries creates a buildup of what James Reason (1990) called "latent failures": faulty elements within the system which no one notices, but which lead to failure in certain conditions. One example: missing information makes precise searching counterproductive. "In any situation where humans use artefacts to accomplish something, the dependability of the artefact is essential" Hollnagel (2002) noted, and "if we cannot rely or depend on the artefact, we cannot really use it."

The probabilistic catalog of automatically generated metadata discussed by Markey (2007) has one particularly important characteristic: nothing in it can be trusted. Wendell Berry noted 30 years ago that the chief product of all industrial processes is garbage, and this is as true with the automatic generation of information as of any other industrial process. Machines, software, algorithms cannot evaluate and judge for they have no values, no commitments to truth, accuracy, honesty, they make no demands for evidence, they have no purposes and no practices. They follow none of Grice's 9 standards for communication. They do not communicate for they have nothing to say. The usefulness, relevance, accuracy, truth, value and potential of any machine generated information can only be determined by a human being who is both capable of making that evaluation and has the resources to do so.

When that human evaluation is not done, when the work has been relegated entirely to an automated process, whether that is bureaucratically or mechanically enforced, the values and practices of science and scholarship—attention, observation, documentation, analysis, argumentation, verification, critique, probing for error, responsibility and accountability—have been eliminated from the library. The library can indeed continue its existence as a group of managers overseeing a technical system, but can it serve the needs of a community whose values it repudiates *in toto*? When the work of libraries is assumed not to involve the building and managing of a collection for the particular needs of a particular community then the work can be performed mechanically or outsourced to the lowest bidder *because the results do not matter*. This is ultimately why Roy Tennant could write of LibraryThing's "Also known as" mechanism that "the quality of this work is only as good as any randomly selected group of people walking down the street would be able to produce." (posting to Autocat, 24 April 2007).

Research libraries have one reason for existing: to serve the needs of research, science and scholarship. To do that it is necessary to understand those practices and the values which unite the communities of researchers, scientists and scholars. And those which divide them: in the first meeting of the Working Group Professor Burke suggested that we might have to forget backward compatibility; that is not something all of us would agree upon. We are not from Mars; like it or not, we are encumbered by history. Much of the existing debate over structures and standards betrays not only a lack of awareness of the diverse needs of science and scholarship but a repudiation of the core values of those practices. All of the characteristics of academic research have been removed from the library in the case of outsourcing, and abolished entirely in mindless copy-cataloging, original cataloging done for data mining rather than research use, and in any and all systems which relegate description, analysis and interpretation to an automated process, whether the automation is technological or bureaucratic.

What has all this to do with structures and standards? Structures and standards do not create, do not interpret, do not evaluate and do not correct information. Structures and standards know nothing of appropriateness and accuracy, of goals and purposes. Therefore structures and standards can just as easily support the creation, recording and distribution of nonsense and misinformation as anything else, something that the examples in the handout clearly demonstrate.

If we acknowledge this, the implications for all kinds of information use and all manner of information management are far reaching. For example, with the 3rd set of questions we were asked to respond to the statement: "Data are created to be processed by applications. We mine data for meaning, merge and manipulate data [etc.]" That is an admirably clear expression of the original sin of LIS. If data are created for processing by application rather than for communication with library users, then we will create and inhabit a kafkaesque bibliographic universe. The user has been abolished in theory and practice, but of course if there is to be any sense in what happens in libraries it will be the library's users that make it, not the managers or the technologies. If on the other hand we create bibliographic information for certain users in order for those users to accomplish their tasks and goals, this will require that we know what those tasks are and how we may facilitate through data structures and standards the performance of those tasks using the tools available to the user. We can choose to understand what happens in libraries according to a theory of transportation in which all data is equal and we simply move it from one place to another, or we can understand work in libraries according to a theory of communication in which we engage readers in conversations about writers and writings, musicians and music, etc. The importance of that choice lies in the fact that we can do either—with radically different consequences.

Structures and standards: questions and responses

Briefly let me respond directly to some of the questions from the background paper.

1. The first set of questions asks what kinds of structures and standards are needed. My response: *Future technological potential will depend on more structured metadata, not less.* The more you want from information technologies, the more you have to put in. The successful use of information technologies used for purposes of communication requires far more standardization than human beings need for interpretation and use. Any ambiguities or multiple uses in the definition of fields will mean that information in these fields can never be retrospectively disambiguated by automatic means. This is a significant problem for both RDA and Dublin Core.

Again, the paper asks: How can we make better use of current structures and standards in meeting both consumer and management user needs? My emphatic response: *Support rather than suppress human intelligence. Bad policies subvert structures and standards.* In many libraries contradictory policies coexist, such as PCC and below minimal level cataloging. Policies which restrict the amount of interpretation and information regardless of the items being described destroy the potential for sharing metadata. Library policies and organizational structures are largely designed to eliminate the exercise of intelligence, acts of interpretation and judgement because these take time and cost money; yet these are precisely the acts upon which all information technologies remain completely dependent because machines do not think, do not interpret, do not make judgements, make no evaluations and know no users.

Again: What relevant communities need to have input and what organizational structures would best support this? *The most demanding needs of the most demanding users must guide all decisions about structures and standards.* Those needs and users will differ from institution to institution.

2. What about controlled data? *Cross language information retrieval and collocation by subject, author or any other field require a controlled vocabulary.* The history of science is a history of controlled vocabulary, even though that vocabulary is argued and altered through time. Topicality is a judgement rooted in an interpretation and no machine has ever engaged in interpretation or in judgement. Neither keyword searching nor relevance ranking collocate anything. No known techniques can replicate the human interpretations and judgements expressed in the subject headings created by human beings. Furthermore, the problems associated with decontextualized language are to a large degree eliminated when controlled vocabularies are also constructed in pre-coordinated strings using a syntax that contextualizes. LCSH is such a system.

Semantic web. Reading Jacques Arsac, Hubert Dreyfus and Roy Harris would make our assessments of these projects much more realistic.

Playing tag: Del.icio.us Flickr. *Subject analysis with LCSH in MARC is tagging.* Even David Weinberger recognizes that. There is a profound lesson to be learned from the success of that other tagging—the kind not done in libraries—but to my knowledge no one has mentioned it. The value and success of tagging is that it is being done by people involved in the creation, study and use of the items being tagged, exactly like the activities which took place in the library at Alexandria as Jochum (1999) described them, exactly like the scientists and naturalists who collect, describe, classify and study plants, stars and cuneiform tablets. In science as in Flickr, the languages and practices are not separate. In our libraries today there is almost always a split between those actively involved in a particular field (e.g. bibliographers) and those creating the metadata. For the most part—music, map and law often being the exceptions—catalogers are hired to catalog whatever comes in the library and no subject knowledge or activity in any field of endeavor is required, expected or encouraged. Catalogers are hired to be metadata specialists without knowing anything in particular about anything at all. Therefore, when they catalog any particular item they may have no stake in the result, no users in mind, no knowledge of how or why anyone might be looking for that item. Wittgenstein insisted that if we have no practices in common, communication becomes impossible, and the divorce between cataloging and reading and research activity is the source of the real difficulties we have with using and making useful LCSH. The disconnect between intellectual involvement and metadata creation is the great failure of our academic libraries. Copy cataloging compounds the problem, and automatic subject analysis is the extreme limit case.

3. Data are created to be processed by applications. ... Are our structures and standards appropriate to this reality? Tomorrow, like today, we can only search for what is in a bibliographic record, not what we hope or dream that someday software will be able to generate from that record. Reliance upon automatic generation or harvesting of metadata must assume that either the bibliographic universe is monolingual—which it is not in our shared databases—or that the software used will be able to perform the necessary acts of interpretation and translation to and from all languages into all others. Futurologists promised that this capacity would be available in 1957 and it continues to be little more than a promise. Heck's remark should be our mantra: "Beware also of what is sometimes said on automated methodologies. Spontaneous generation of knowledge does not exist as no methodology will ever reveal knowledge that is not already somehow in the data." (Heck, 2001, p.11)

4. On mass digitization: *The more technologically dependent the resources, the more access will cost.* Comparisons between bibliographic records for print and electronic resources suggest that the metadata required for electronic resources is at least double that required for print materials. The single field for physical characteristics in a record for a print item is multiplied many times in the record for an electronic resource—especially for items in physical formats which have been digitized—since the record must include url, indications of type of file, system requirements, rights and restrictions, and a vast array of notes needed for future tasks of digital preservation, interoperability, and much else. Karen Coyle (2007a) quoted Dan Clancy in her blog from the first meeting: "The cost of asserting opinions determines value." Google

relies heavily on metadata because metadata represents cost, i.e. value.

On offsite storage. *Classified shelving is a form of metadata.* Classified shelving is one of the most important structures facilitating access in a library, and it is being eliminated in many instances on the assumption that the online catalog can take over that function. Offsite storage, closed stacks and stacks arranged by accession number severely reduce the information that would be available to the patron in an open classified stacks. Shelving by accession number renders useless half the subject information usually present in a bibliographic record: the class number. Both the information imparted by classified shelving and the learning which it enables are lost when access to bibliographic information is restricted to the online catalog record. If libraries are going to pursue offsite storage, closed stacks and accession number (or bin number) shelving, then far more information will need to be entered into the bibliographic record for *all* users, including the managers, something Andrew Pace indicated in his list of desiderata for the catalog.

5. Libraries now manage different flows of data, created within different regimes, much of it outside the library environment. ... At the same time, we see more reuse and flow of data across publishers, libraries, agents, other bibliographic services, etc. What does this mean for our bibliographic structures and standards? *It does not mean anything if you do not look at it, pay attention, and think about what information the library and its users need.* Breure (2005) referred to reusability as the Holy Grail of content engineering and noted that it "requires that digital information be well structured ... and enriched with metadata ... Most of the strategies to achieve that purpose require special, highly controlled procedures for creating content." (p. 27) Unfortunately, Breure concluded, "the majority of content is created without the strict procedures that enable reuse." (p. 47)

Conclusion

Consider again Grice's standards for communication:

1. Make your contribution as informative as is required
2. Do not make your contribution more informative than is required
3. Do not say what you believe to be false
4. Do not say that for which you lack adequate evidence
5. Be relevant
6. Avoid obscurity of expression
7. Avoid ambiguity
8. Be brief
9. Be orderly

Without human devotion to communication along the lines Grice outlined, without attention, evaluation, interpretation, correction and adaptation for the intended users of the information, all the structures and standards in the world will produce nothing but meaningless nonsense. If we want information appropriate to our users' needs and practices, we have to create it to fit those needs and practices: it does not exist otherwise.

Bibliography

(The bibliography includes not only the works cited in the paper as read May 9th, but additional material which was discussed in a longer version circulated earlier. The additional references are to studies of reliability and error in technical systems from the perspectives of ergonomics and management.)

Ashby, William Ross (1956). *Introduction to cybernetics.* London: Chapman & Hall. Available on line at: http://pespmc1.vub.ac.be/books/IntroCyb.pdf

Bainbridge, Lisanne (1987). "Ironies of automation." In: J. Rasmussen et al. *New technology and human error,* New York: Wiley. p. 271-283.

Breure, Leen (2005). "Reuse of content and digital genres" in: Herre van Oostendorp, Leen Breure and Andrew Dillon, *Creation, use, and deployment of digital information*. Mahwah, NJ: Lawrence Erlbaum Associates. p.27-53.

Burrows, Howard; Suresh, Ramachandran (1998). "Digital library aproaches to resource discovery in earth and space science" in: Strobl, J. and Best, C. (Eds.), *Proceedings of the Earth Observation & Geo-Spatial Web and Internet Workshop '98 = Salzburger Geographische Materialien*, Volume 27. Available at: http://www.sbg.ac.at/geo/eogeo/authors/burrows/burrows.htm

Calhoun, Karen (2003). "Technology, productivity and change in library technical services" *Library collections, acquisitions, & technical services* v.27 p.281-289.

Coyle, Karen (2007a). Users and uses: Google Scholar. Available at: http://kcoyle.blogspot.com/2007/03/users-and-uses-google-scholar.html

Coyle, Karen (2007b). Users and uses: Karen's summary. Available at: http://kcoyle.blogspot.com/2007/03/users-and-uses-karens-summary.html

Coyle, Karen (2007c). Users and uses: official summary. Available at: http://kcoyle.blogspot.com/2007/03/users-and-uses-official-summary.html

De Keyser, Véronique (1990). "Temporal decision making in complex environments" *Philosophical transactions of the Royal Society of London. SeriesB: Biological sciences*, v.327, no.1241, *Human factors in hazardous situations* (Apr. 12, 1990), p. 569-576.

Denis, Hélène (2005). "Les risques et les catastrophes" In: Minguet and Thuderoz (eds.), *Travail, entreprise et société: manuel de sociologie pour ingénieurs et scientifiques*. Paris: PUF, p.68-80.

Dörner, Dietrich (1997). *The logic of failure: recognizing and avoiding error in complex situations*. Reading, Mass: Addison-Wesley. Translation of *Die Logik des Mißlingens*.

Dupuy, Jean-Pierre (1980). "Analyse de systèmes et critique de la société 'informationnelle.'" In: F. Gallouedec-Genuys, ed., *Les enjeux culturels de l'informatisation.* Fontefraud: Centre Culturel de l'Ouest. p. 183-201.

Fallgren, Nancy J. (2007a). *Users and uses of bibliographic data: background paper for the Working Group on the Future of Bibliographic Control.* Available at: http://www.loc.gov/bibliographic-future/meetings/docs/UsersandUsesBackgroundPaper.pdf

Fallgren, Nancy J. (2007b). *Users and Uses of Bibliographic Data Meeting March 8, 2007 Mountain View, CA: brief meeting summary.* Available at: http://www.loc.gov/bibliographic-future/meetings/2007_mar08.html

Fallgren, Nancy J. (2007c). *Structures and standards for bibliographic data: background paper for the Working Group on the Future of Bibliographic Control.* Available at: http://www.loc.gov/bibliographic-future/meetings/docs/mtg2paperfinal2.pdf

Gras, Alain; avec Sophie L. Poirot-Delpech (1993). *Grandeur et dépendance: sociologie des macro-systèmes techniques.* Paris: PUF.

Grice, H.P. (1975). "Logic and conversation" in P. Cole and J. Morgan, *Syntax and semantics,* v.3: *Speech acts.* New York: Academic Press, p. 41-58.

Heck, André (2001). "Information handling in astronomy: beyond technologies and methodologies" *High energy physics libraries webzine,* issue 3 (March). Available at: http://library.cern.ch/HEPLW/3/papers/2/

Hjørland, Birger (1997). *Information seeking and subject representation:an activity-theoretical approach to information science.* Westport, Conn.:Greenwood Press.

Hollnagel, Erik (2002). "Dependability of joint human-computer systems," in S. Anderson et al., eds., *Computer safety, reliability and security: 21st International Conference, SAFECOMP 2002, Catania, Italy, September 10-13.* (Berlin: Springer, 2002; Lecture notes in computer science, v.2434), p. 4-9.

Hollnagel, Erik; Woods, David D. (2005). *Joint cognitive systems: foundations of cognitive systems engineering.* Boca Raton: CRC.

Jochum, Uwe (1999). "The Alexandrian Library and its aftermath" Library history v.15 p.5-12.

Landau, M.; Stout, R. (1979). "To manage is not to control, or the folly of type II errors" *Public administration review* v.39 nr.2 (March-April), p.148-156.

Langer, Ellen J. (1989). "Minding matters: the consequences of mindlessness-mindfulness" *Advances in experimental social psychology* v.22 p.137-173.

"Law of Requisite Variety," in *Web Dictionary of Cybernetics and Systems* http://pespmc1.vub.ac.be/ASC/LAW_VARIE.html (viewed 8 May 2007)

Markey, Karen (2007). "The online library catalog: Paradise Lost and Paradise Regained?" *D-Lib Magazine* v. 13 nr.1/2 (January/February). Available at: http://www.dlib.org/dlib/january07/markey/01markey.html

Marsh, Stephen; Dibben, Mark R. (2003). "The role of trust in information science and technology" *Annual review of information science and technology* v.37 p.465-498.

Morel, Christian (2003). *Les décisions absurdes: sociologie des erreurs radicales et persistantes.* Paris: nrf Gallimard.

Naumann, Felix; Rolker, Claudia (1999). "Do metadata models meet IQ requirements?" In: *Proceedings of the International Conference on Information Quality 1999 (IQ'99), MIT.* Available at: http://hqiq.de/publications.html

Norman, Donald A. (1990). *The design of everyday things.* New York: Doubleday.

Orlikowski, Wanda J. (1991). "Integrated information environment or matrix of control? The contradictory implications of information technology" *Accounting, management and information technology* v.1 no.1 p.9-42.

Poyet, Christine (1990). "L'homme, agent de fiabilité dans les systèmes automatisés." In: Leplat and Terssac, eds., *Les facteurs humains de la fiabilité dans les systèmes complexes*, p.223-240.

Reason, James (1990). *Human error.* New York: Cambridge University Press.

Sperber, Dan; Wilson, Deirdre (1986). *Relevance: communication and cognition.* Cambridge: Harvard University Press.

Tennant, Roy (2007). "LibraryThing and FRBR entities." Posting to Autocat, 24 April 2007.

Townsend, Robert (2007). *Google Books: What's not to like?* Posted 30 April on *AHA today*, the AHA blog. Available at: http://blog.historians.org/articles/204/google-books-whats-not-to-like

Truitt, Marc (2006). "On 'earth-shaking matters'…" Posting to Autocat, 30 August 2006.

Vestrucci, Paolo (1990). *Modelli per la valutazione dell'affidabilità umana.* Milano: Franco Angeli.

Weick, Karl E.; Sutcliffe, Kathleen M. (2001). *Managing the unexpected: assuring high performance in an age of complexity.* San Francisco: Jossey-Bass.

Woods, David D.; Johannsen, Leila J.; Cook, Richard I.; Sarter, Nadine B. (1994). *Behind human error: cognitive systems, computers, and hindsight.* Wright Patterson AFB, Ohio: CSERIAC.

Appendix/Handout

The following ten examples of bibliographic records found in OCLC (before and after correction) clearly demonstrate problems in the organizational infrastructure for creating and maintaining bibliographic information in an environment of different flows of data, created within different regimes, some of it outside the library environment. Printouts of each record as I found it in OCLC are reproduced in the pages that follow, and for each one I have also printed out the revised record.

Examples 1-3. Bibliographic records contributed to OCLC by book seller.

1. (This example is discussed in the talk.)

2. A book in the Albanian language, it is described in the fixed fields (the searchable field) as Ukrainian, and in the note field as Azerbaijani. The fixed field for country of publication has Ukraine, but the book is published in Albania. The wrong diacritic appears in the form of name. The English title does not appear on the book. The subjects given are so general as to be of no use in subject searching.

3. Again a book in the Albanian language published in Albania but described as a Russian book in both language and country of publication fields. Author's name appears in reverse order in the statement of responsibility, unlike it appears on the book. Physical description is wrong (pagination) and incomplete (dimensions). The imprint date is given as unknown in the fixed fields and 2000? in the imprint. Diacritics missing in the title and imprint, while again the English title does not appear on the book and the subjects given are so general as to be of no use in subject searching.

Examples 4-5. Bibliographic records created for data mining

4. Aside from the lack of information, the book is described as being in English and having no place of publication in the fixed fields. (Note, 4 Sept. 2007: I have since learned that this record and many like it were not intended for data mining at all, but were simply the result of

batchloads gone wrong which no one noticed until someone from outside the batchloading institution notified the latter of the problem. While this means that this example does not belong under this heading, it is an example whose history is now known and therefore one from which much can be learned, if only we pay attention.)

5. The fixed fields are those of the default settings rather than based upon the book. The class number is for modern Russian literature in relation to Italy (Class web note: "Class here works dealing with the influence of foreign authors on Russian literature if written chiefly in the interest of Russian literature"). The title in the record is taken from the t.p. verso, not from the title page. That title says "in 2 books" and the record itself is based on volume 2 but the dates and physical description fields indicate further volumes will be published. The nature of the book, the presence of translations, Petrarch as author and subject, and vernacular data are all missing.

Examples 6-7. Bibliographic records in OCLC supplied by large research libraries

6. According to ClassWeb the classification number is for "European Union in relation to individual regions or countries" with .R8 for Russia which matches the 3rd and 4th subjects given. However the book is not about Russia at all: the title translated is Europe without Russia: the Treaty Establishing a Constitution for Europe of 20 October 2004. It is a translation of that treaty into Russian with an essay by Václav Klaus, and should be classed KJE (European Union constitutional law). Vernacular data not included.

7. The class number and the subject headings match, but they are all wrong.

Example 8. Copy-cataloging with neither evaluation nor correction

8. Again no vernacular data. Author mistakenly identified as subject of a congress (in fixed fields), but class number based on the additional and also completely wrong subjects for Slavic peoples, ethnography (general). Records from all of the holding libraries indicate that none of these problems were identified or corrected.

APPENDIX   139

Examples 9-10. PCC records in OCLC

9. Class number and subject headings for Romania--Ethnography--General works. A note mentions volume 4, which has not been published yet, and the library's catalog indicates that only volume 1 is owned. According to the introduction of this multivolume book it will be devoted entirely to reporting on the responses to a questionnaire about habitat (domestic spaces) of the living and the dead in Romania, each volume concerning a particular region. It is not folklore.

10. A guidebook to archives of Polish institutions abroad. It is not the archives themselves, as the 6th subject heading indicates. Without making corrections LC accepted this record into its catalog where a 985 field states "VENDOR LOAD." What is really interesting here is that a record created by the National Library of Poland is also available in OCLC and in that record the correct subject headings are given, albeit in Polish. LC did not use copy-cataloging or data mining to find the good record (adapting it for an English language catalog) nor to correct the bad record, but instead accepted the incorrect record and made no corrections.

Example 1:1

Rec stat n	Entered 20051018		Replaced 20051102		
Type a	ELvl M	Srce d	Audn	Ctrl	Lang rus
BLvl m	Form	Conf 0	Biog	MRec	Ctry ru
	Cont	GPub	LitF 0	Indx 0	
Desc a	Ills	Fest 0	DtSt s	Dates uuuu ,	

040	EVIEW ǂb eng ǂc EVIEW
020	9994362828 : ǂc USD31.95
029 0	EVIEW ǂb J2001627
090	ǂb
049	CGUA
100 1	Varfri, M.
245 0 0	Fjalor lokucionesh Frengjisht-Shqip = ǂb French - Albanian Idioms Dictionary / ǂc Varfri, M.
260	Tirana : ǂb Albatros, ǂc [2000?]
300	256 p. ; ǂc cm.
546	In Russian ǂb (roman)
650 0 4	Humanities.
650 0 4	Languages/linguistics.
650 0 4	Albania.
938	East View Publications ǂb EAST ǂn J2001627 ǂc USD31.95

Delete Holdings-   Export- Label- Produce- Submit- Replace- Report Error-   Update Holdings-   Validate- Workflow-In Process

Example 1:2

Rec stat n	Entered 20051018		Replaced 20051102		
Type a	ELvl	Srce c	Audn	Ctrl	Lang alb
BLvl m	Form	Conf 0	Biog	MRec	Ctry aa
	Cont d	GPub	LitF 0	Indx 0	
Desc a	Ills	Fest 0	DtSt s	Dates 2004 ,	

040		EVIEW ‡b eng ‡c EVIEW
020		9994362828
029	0	EVIEW ‡b J2001627
041	0	alb ‡a fre
042		pcc
050	4	PG9593 ‡b .V374 2004
090		‡b
049		CGUA
100	1	Varfi, Nonda.
245	1 0	Fjalor lokucionesh frëngjisht-shqip / ‡c Nonda Varfi, Viktor Z. Bakillari.
260		Tiranë : ‡b Albatros, ‡c 2004.
300		252 p. ; ‡c 21 cm.
650	0	French language ‡x Idioms ‡v Dictionaries ‡x Albanian.
650	0	French language ‡v Dictionaries ‡x Albanian.
700	1	Bakillari, Viktor Z.
938		East View Publications ‡b EAST ‡n J2001627 ‡c USD31.95

Delete Holdings- Source-OCLC   Export- C   Label- Produce- Submit- Replace- Report Error-   Update Holdings-   Validate-C Workflow-In Process

Example 2:1

Rec stat n	Entered 20051003		Replaced 20051102		
Type a	ELvl M	Srce d	Audn	Ctrl	Lang ukr
BLvl m	Form	Conf 0	Biog	MRec	Ctry un
	Cont	GPub	LitF 0	Indx 0	
Desc a	Ills	Fest 0	DtSt s	Dates 2005 ,	

```
040      EVIEW ǂb eng ǂc EVIEW
020      9994331590 : ǂc USD25.95
029 0    EVIEW ǂb J2001607
090      ǂb
049      CGUA
100 1    Ko<F7>ço, Eno.
245 0 0  Shostakovic dhe Kadare & artikuj, profile, intervista e vrojtime mbi artin muzikor shqiptar = ǂb
         Shostakovich and Kadare & articles, profiles, interviews and observations over Albanian musica
         art / ǂc Koço, Eno.
260      Tirana : ǂb Uegen, ǂc 2005.
300      200 p. ; ǂc cm.
546      In Azerbaijani ǂb (roman)
650 0 4  Humanities.
650 0 4  Music.
650 0 4  Albania.
938      East View Publications ǂb EAST ǂn J2001607 ǂc USD25.95
```

Delete Holdings-	Export- Label- Produce- Submit- Replace- Report Error-	Update Holdings-	Validate- Workflow-In Process

APPENDIX

Example 2:2

Rec stat c	Entered 20051003		Replaced 20061024		
Type a	ELvl	Srce c	Audn	Ctrl	Lang alb
BLvl m	Form	Conf 0	Biog	MRec	Ctry aa
	Cont b	GPub	LitF 0	Indx 0	
Desc a	Ills	Fest 0	DtSt s	Dates 2005 ,	

040		EVIEW ‡b eng ‡c EVIEW ‡d CGU
020		9994331590
029 0		EVIEW ‡b J2001607
041 1		alb ‡h eng
042		pcc
043		e-aa---
050	4	ML3601.1 ‡b .K636 2005
090		‡b
049		CGUA
100 1		Koço, Eno.
245 1 0		Shostakovic dhe Kadare : ‡b & artikuj, profile, intervista e vrojtime mbi artin muzikor shqiptar / ‡c Eno Koço.
260		Tirana : ‡b Uegen, ‡c 2005.
300		200 p. ; ‡c 21 cm.
504		Includes bibliographical references.
650	0	Music ‡z Albania ‡x History.
650	0	World War, 1939-1945 ‡z Albania ‡x Music and the war.
650	0	Music and war ‡z Albania.
600 1 0		Kadare, Ismail.
600 1 0		Shostakovich, Dmitriĭ Dmitrievich, ‡d 1906-1975.
600 1 0		Koço, Eno ‡v Interviews.
938		East View Publications ‡b EAST ‡n J2001607 ‡c USD25.95

Delete Holdings-   Export- Label- Produce- Submit- Replace- Report Error-   Update Holdings-   Validate- Workflow-In Process

Example 3:1

Rec stat n	Entered 20051018		Replaced 20051102		
Type a	ELvl M	Srce d	Audn	Ctrl	Lang rus
BLvl m	Form	Conf 0	Biog	MRec	Ctry ru
	Cont	GPub	LitF 0	Indx 0	
Desc a	Ills	Fest 0	DtSt s	Dates uuuu ,	

```
040        EVIEW ǂb eng ǂc EVIEW
020        9994373374 : ǂc USD28.95
029 0      EVIEW ǂb J2001624
090        ǂb
049        CGUA
100 1      Qosja, Rexhep.
245 0 0    Shkrimtare dhe perudha = ǂb Writers and Periods / ǂc Qosja, Rexhep.
260        Tirana : ǂb Akademia, ǂc [2000?]
300        586 p. ; ǂc cm.
546        In Russian ǂb (roman)
650 0 4    Humanities.
650 0 4    Literary criticism.
650 0 4    Albania.
938        East View Publications ǂb EAST ǂn J2001624 ǂc USD28.95
```

Delete Holdings- | Export- Label- Produce- Submit- Replace- Report Error- | Update Holdings- | Validate- Workflow-In Process

APPENDIX

Example 3:2

Rec stat n	Entered 20061020		Replaced 20061020		
Type a	ELvl	Srce c	Audn	Ctrl	Lang alb
BLvl m	Form	Conf 0	Biog	MRec	Ctry aa
	Cont b	GPub	LitF 0	Indx 1	
Desc a	Ills	Fest 0	DtSt s	Dates 2005 ,	

040		CGU ǂc CGU
020		9994373374
020		9789994373376
042		pcc
043		e-aa---
050	4	PG9606 ǂb .Q28 2005
090		ǂb
049		CGUA
100	1	Qosja, Rexhep.
245	1 0	Shkrimtarë dhe periudha / ǂc Rexhep Qosja.
260		Tiranë : ǂb Akademia e Shkencave e Shqipërisë, ǂc 2005.
300		585 p. ; ǂc 22 cm.
504		Includes bibliographical references and index.
650	0	Albanian literature ǂy 20th century ǂx History and criticism.
650	0	Albanian literature ǂx Periodization.

Delete Export- Label- Produce- Submit- Replace- Report Update Validate-
Holdings-   Error- Holdings-
                                                         Workflow-In
                                                         Process

Example 4

Rec stat n	Entered 20061208		Replaced 20070221		
Type a	ELvl M	Srce d	Audn	Ctrl	Lang eng
BLvl m	Form	Conf 0	Biog	MRec	Ctry xx
	Cont	GPub	LitF 0	Indx 0	
Desc	Ills	Fest 0	DtSt s	Dates 2006 ,	

```
040      N15 ǂc N15
020      5981871415
020      9785981871412
090      ǂb
049      CGUA
100 1    IUSUPOVA, T.I.
245 1 0  MONGOL'SKAIA KOMISSIIA AKADEMII NAUK ǂb ISTORIIA SOZDANIIA I DEIATEL'NOSTI.
260      SPB ǂb NESTOR-ISTORIIA ǂc 2006.
```

Delete Holdings-   Export- Label- Produce- Submit- Replace- Report Error-   Update Holdings-   Validate- Workflow-In Process

APPENDIX 147

Example 5:1

Rec stat n	Entered 20061115		Replaced 20070223			
Type a	ELvl 3	Srce d	Audn	Ctrl	Lang rus	
BLvl m	Form	Conf 0	Biog	MRec	Ctry ru	
	Cont	GPub	LitF 0	Indx 0		
Desc a	Ills	Fest 0	DtSt s	Dates 2006 ,	9999	

040		COO ‡c COO
020		5738002253
020		9785738002250
050	4	PG2981.I8 ‡b P47 2006
090		‡b
049		CGUA
245	0 0	Petrarka v russkoĭ literature v 2-kh knigakh / ‡c [sost. V.T. Danchenko].
246	1 3	Petrarca nella literatura russa
260		Moskva : ‡b Rudomino, ‡c 2006-
300		v. ; ‡c 24 cm.
653		Literature, Comparative ‡a Russian and Italian.
700	1	Danchenko, V. T.

Delete Holdings-   Export- Label- Produce- Submit- Replace- Report Error-   Update Holdings-   Validate- Workflow-In Process

Example 5:2

Rec stat c	Entered 20061115		Replaced 20070417			
Type a	ELvl	Srce c	Audn	Ctrl		Lang rus
BLvl m	Form	Conf 0	Biog d	MRec o		Ctry ru
	Cont b	GPub	LitF m	Indx 0		
Desc a	Ills a	Fest 0	DtSt s	Dates 2006 ,		

```
040        COO ǂc COO ǂd CGU
066        ǂc (N
020        5738002083 (kn. 1)
020        9785738002083 (kn. 1)
020        5738002253 (kn. 2)
020        9785738002250 (kn. 2)
041 1      rus ǂh ita
042        pcc
043        e-ru---
050     4  PQ4537.R8 ǂb P48 2006
049        CGUA
⌈245 0 0   Петрарка в русской литературе / ǂc [сост. В.Т. Данченко].
⌊245 0 0   Petrarka v russkoĭ literature / ǂc [sost. V.T. Danchenko].
246 1 5    Petrarca nella literatura russa
⌈260       Москва : ǂb Рудомино, ǂc 2006.
⌊260       Moskva : ǂb Rudomino, ǂc 2006.
300        2 v. : ǂb ill. ; ǂc 24 cm.
500        Collected translations, critical essays and notes on Petrarch by Russian authors, 1752-2003.
504        Includes bibliographical references.
600 1 0    Petrarca, Francesco, ǂd 1304-1374 ǂx Appreciation ǂz Russia.
600 1 0    Petrarca, Francesco, ǂd 1304-1374 ǂx Appreciation ǂz Russia (Federation)
600 1 0    Petrarca, Francesco, ǂd 1304-1374 ǂv Translations into Russian.
600 1 0    Petrarca, Francesco, ǂd 1304-1374 ǂx Criticism and interpretation.
650     0  Literature, Comparative ǂx Russian and Italian.
650     0  Literature, Comparative ǂx Italian and Russian.
700 1      Petrarca, Francesco, ǂd 1304-1374.
⌈700 1     Данченко, В. Т.
⌊700 1     Danchenko, V. T.
```

| Delete Holdings- | Export- C | Label- | Produce- | Submit- C | Replace- | Report Error- | Update Holdings- | Validate-C Workflow-In Process |

APPENDIX

Example 6:1

Rec stat n	Entered 20060627		Replaced 20060627		
Type a	ELvl I	Srce d	Audn	Ctrl	Lang rus
BLvl m	Form	Conf 0	Biog	MRec o	Ctry ru
	Cont b	GPub	LitF 0	Indx 0	
Desc a	Ills	Fest 0	DtSt s	Dates 2005,	

040		ZCU ǂc ZCU
020		5973900061
043		e------ ǂa e-ru---
050	4	HC240.25.R8 ǂb E97 2005
090		ǂb
049		CGUA
245	0 0	Evropa bez Rossii : ǂb dogovor, uchrezhdai͡u͡shchiĭ Konstitut͡s͡ii͡u͡ dli͡a͡ Evropy ot 20 okti͡a͡bri͡a͡ 2004 goda / ǂc [perevod s angliĭskogo O. Dubit͡s͡kai͡a͡ ... et al.].
246	1	ǂi Title on p. 17: ǂa Dogovor, uchrezhdai͡u͡shchiĭ konstitut͡s͡ii͡u͡ dli͡a͡ Evropy
260		Moskva : ǂb Izd-vo "Evropa", ǂc 2005.
300		573 p. ; ǂc 20 cm.
440	0	Serii͡a͡ "Mirovoĭ pori͡a͡dok"
504		Includes bibliographical references.
610	2 0	European Union ǂv Constitution.
650	0	Constitutional law ǂz European Union countries.
651	0	European Union countries ǂx Relations ǂz Russia (Federation)
651	0	Russia (Federation) ǂx Relations ǂz European Union countries.
700	1	Dubit͡s͡kai͡a͡, O.
730	0 2	Treaty Establishing a Constitution for Europe ǂd (2004). ǂl Russian.

Delete Holdings-	Export- Label- Produce- Submit- Replace- Report Error-	Update Holdings-	Validate- Workflow-In Process

Example 6:2

Rec stat c	Entered 20060627		Replaced 20061017		
Type a	ELvl	Srce c	Audn	Ctrl	Lang rus
BLvl m	Form	Conf 0	Biog	MRec o	Ctry ru
	Cont b	GPub	LitF 0	Indx 0	
Desc a	Ills	Fest 0	DtSt s	Dates 2005 ,	

```
040        ZCU ǂc ZCU ǂd CGU
066        ǂc (N
020        5973900061
041 1      rus ǂh cze ǂh cze
042        pcc
043        e-----
050    4   KJE4443.32004 ǂb .A2 2005a
049        CGUA
130 0      Treaty Establishing a Constitution for Europe ǂd (2004). ǂl Russian.
┌245 1 0   Европа без России : ǂb Договор, учреждающий Конституцию для Европы от 20 октября
│              2004 года / ǂc [перевод с английского О. Дубицкая ... ет ал.].
└245 1 0   Evropa bez Rossii : ǂb Dogovor, uchrezhdai͡u͡shchiĭ Konstitut͡s͡ii͡u͡ dli͡a͡ Evropy ot 20
               okti͡a͡bri͡a͡ 2004 goda / ǂc [perevod s angliĭskogo O. Dubit͡s͡kai͡a͡ ... et al.].
┌246 1 0   Договор, учреждающий конституцию для Европы
└246 1 0   Dogovor, uchrezhdai͡u͡shchiĭ konstitut͡s͡ii͡u͡ dli͡a͡ Evropy
┌260       Москва : ǂb Европа, ǂc 2005.
└260       Moskva : ǂb Evropa, ǂc 2005.
300        573 p. ; ǂc 20 cm.
┌490 1     Мировой порядок
└490 1     Mirovoĭ pori͡a͡dok
┌500       Includes "Почему я не "европеист"" (translated from Czech) by Václav Klaus (p. 9-16).
└500       Includes "Pochemu i͡a͡ ne "evropeist"" (translated from Czech) by Václav Klaus (p. 9-16).
504        Includes bibliographical references (p. 16).
610 2 0    European Union ǂv Constitution.
650    0   Constitutions ǂz European Union countries.
650    0   Constitutional law ǂz European Union countries.
┌700 1     Дубицкая, О.
└700 1     Dubit͡s͡kai͡a͡, O.
700 1      Klaus, Václav.
┌830 0     Серия "Мировой порядок".
└830 0     Serii͡a͡ "Mirovoĭ pori͡a͡dok".
```

APPENDIX

Example 7:1

Rec stat	n	Entered 20061116		Replaced 20070116			
Type	a	ELvl K	Srce d	Audn	Ctrl	Lang	por
BLvl	m	Form	Conf 0	Biog	MRec	Ctry	bl
		Cont	GPub	LitF 0	Indx 0		
Desc	a	Ills	Fest 0	DtSt s	Dates 2006 ,		

040		AZU ǂc AZU
020		8575262068
020		9788575262061
090		HN283.5 ǂb .M314 2006
090		ǂb
049		CGUA
100	1	Mafra, Rennan.
245	1 0	Entre o espetáculo, a festa e a argumentação : ǂb mídia, comunicação estratégica e mobilização social / ǂc Rennan Mafra.
260		Belo Horizonte : ǂb Autêntica, ǂc 2006.
300		191 p. ; ǂc 21 cm.
440	0	Comunicação e mobilização social ; ǂv 4.
500		Includes bibliographical references.
650	0	Social Movements ǂz Brazil.
651	0	Brazil ǂx Social conditions.

Delete Holdings-   Export- Label- Produce- Submit- Replace- Report Error-   Update Holdings-   Validate- Workflow-In Process

Example 7:2

Rec stat	c	Entered 20061116		Replaced 20070212		
Type	a	ELvl	Srce c	Audn	Ctrl	Lang por
BLvl	m	Form	Conf 0	Biog	MRec	Ctry bl
		Cont b	GPub	LitF 0	Indx 0	
Desc	a	Ills	Fest 0	DtSt s	Dates 2006 ,	

```
040        AZU ǂc AZU ǂd CGU
020        8575262068
020        9788575262061
042        pcc
043        s-bl---
050     4  P96.P832 ǂb M34 2006
090        ǂb
049        CGUA
100  1     Mafra, Rennan.
245  1  0  Entre o espetáculo, a festa e a argumentação : ǂb mídia, comunicação estratégica e
           mobilização social / ǂc Rennan Mafra.
260        Belo Horizonte : ǂb Autêntica, ǂc 2006.
300        191 p. ; ǂc 21 cm.
440     0  Comunicação e mobilização social ; ǂv 4.
504        Includes bibliographical references.
610  2  0  Projeto Manuelzão.
610  2  0  Expedição Manuelzão Desce o Rio das Velhas.
650     0  Mass media and public opinion ǂz Brazil ǂv Case studies.
650     0  Environmental management ǂz Brazil ǂx Citizen participation.
650     0  Regional planning ǂz Brazil ǂx Citizen participation.
650     0  Communication in regional planning ǂz Brazil.
650     0  Scientific expeditions ǂz Brazil.
```

Delete Holdings-	Export- Label- Produce- Submit- Replace- Report Error-	Update Holdings-	Validate- Workflow-In Process

APPENDIX

Example 8:1

Rec stat n	Entered 20061108		Replaced 20070225		
Type a	ELvl I	Srce d	Audn	Ctrl	Lang rus
BLvl m	Form	Conf 1	Biog	MRec o	Ctry ru
	Cont b	GPub	LitF 0	Indx 0	
Desc a	Ills o	Fest 0	DtSt s	Dates 2006,	

040	SU ǂc OSU
020	157602015
020	985757602011
090	DK27 ǂb .S54 2006
090	ǂ
049	GUA
245 0 0	Slavi︠a︡nskiĭ mir : ǂb problemy istorii i sovremennostʹ (pami︠a︡ti Vladimira Konstantinovicha Vŏlkova) / ǂc [otvetstv. redaktor A.V. Karasev].
260	Moskva : ǂb Institut slavi︠a︡novedenii︠a︡ RAN, ǂc 2006.
300	14 p. : ǂb ill. ; ǂc 21 cm.
500	Ahead of title: Pravitelʹstvo Moskvy. Komitet mezhregionalʹnykh svi︠a︡zeĭ i nat︠s︡ionalʹnoĭ politiki g.Moskvy. Rossiĭskai︠a︡ akademii︠a︡ nauk. Institut slavi︠a︡novedenii︠a︡. Slavi︠a︡nskiĭ fond Rossii.
500	"Nauchnoe izdanie"--Colophon.
504	Includes bibliographical references.
600 1 0	Volkov, V. K. ǂq (Vladimir Konstantinovich)
650 0	Slavs ǂx Antiquities.
650 0	Civilization, Slavic.
700 1	Karasev, A.V.

Delete Holdings-   Export- Label- Produce- Submit- Replace- Report Error-   Update Holdings-   Validate- Workflow-In Process

Example 8:2

```
ec stat c     Entered 20061108    Replaced 20070227
ype a         El.vl        Srce c    Audn         Ctrl          Lang rus
Lvl m         Form         Conf 0    Biog d       MRec o        Ctry ru
              Cont b       GPub      LitF 0       Indx 0
esc a         Ills   a     Fest 0    DtSt s       Dates 2006 ,
```

```
040           OSU ǂc OSU ǂd CGU
066           ǂc (N
020           5757602015
020           9785757602011
042           pcc
043           ed---- ǂa e-yu--- ǂa e-ru---
050      4    DR3 ǂb .V655 2006
090           ǂb
049           CGUA
100  1        Волков, В. К. ǂq (Владимир Константинович)
100  1        Volkov, V. K. ǂq (Vladimir Konstantinovich)
245  1 0      Славянский мир : ǂb проблемы истории и современность (памяти Владимира
              Константиновича Волкова) / ǂc [ответств. редактор А.В. Карасев].
245  1 0      Slavi︠a︡nskiĭ mir : ǂb problemy istorii i sovremennostʹ (pami︠a︡ti Vladimira Konstantinovicha
              Volkova) / ǂc [otvetstv. redaktor A.V. Karasev].
260           Москва : ǂb Институт славяноведения РАН, ǂc 2006.
260           Moskva : ǂb Institut slavi︠a︡novedenii︠a︡ RAN, ǂc 2006.
300           134 p., [8] p. of plates : ǂb ill. ; ǂc 21 cm.
500           At head of title: Правительство Москвы. Комитет межрегиональных связей и национальной
              политики г. Москвы. Российская академия наук. Институт славяноведения. Славянский
              фонд России.
500           At head of title: Pravitelʹstvo Moskvy. Komitet mezhregionalʹnykh svi︠a︡zeĭ i nat︠s︡ionalʹnoĭ
              politiki g. Moskvy. Rossiĭskai︠a︡ akademii︠a︡ nauk. Institut slavi︠a︡novedenii︠a︡. Slavi︠a︡nskiĭ
              fond Rossii.
504           Includes bibliographical references.
505  0 0      ǂt Памяти Владимира Константиновича Волкова (1930-2005) -- ǂt Сербия: 200 лет борьбы
              -- ǂt Вторая мировая война и славянские народы (некоторые размышления в связи с 50-
              летием Победы) -- ǂt Балканы в системе геополитических интересов России -- ǂt
              Балканская западня и проблема столкновения цивилизаций -- ǂt Трагедия Югославии
              (1991-1995) -- ǂt Российская историческая славистика на пороге XXI века: смена
              исследовательской парадигмы -- ǂt "Славянская идея" и русское национальное
              самосознание.
505  0 0      ǂt Pami︠a︡ti Vladimira Konstantinovicha Volkova (1930-2005) -- ǂt Serbii︠a︡: 200 let borʹby --
```

Example 8:3

‡t Vtorai͡a mirovai͡a voĭna i slavi͡anskie narody (nekotorye razmyshlenii͡a v svi͡azi s 50-letiem Pobedy) -- ‡t Balkany v sisteme geopoliticheskikh interesov Rossii -- ‡t Balkanskai͡a zapadni͡a i problema stolknovenii͡a t͡sivilizat͡siĭ -- ‡t Tragedii͡a I͡Ugoslavii (1991-1995) -- ‡t Rossiĭskai͡a istoricheskai͡a slavistika na poroge XXI veka: smena issledovatel'skoĭ paradigmy -- ‡t "Slavi͡anskai͡a idei͡a" i russkoe nat͡sional'noe samosoznanie.

1	0	Balkan Peninsula ‡x History ‡y 20th century.
1	0	Serbia ‡x History, Military.
)	0	Yugoslav War, 1991-1995.
)	0	Slavophilism.
)	0	World War, 1939-1945 ‡z Soviet Union.
	0	Balkan Peninsula ‡x Foreign relations ‡z Russia (Federation)
	0	Russia (Federation) ‡x Foreign relations ‡z Balkan Peninsula.
1	0	Волков, В. К. ‡q (Владимир Константинович)
1	0	Volkov, V. K. ‡q (Vladimir Konstantinovich)
1		Карасев, А. В.
1		Karasev, A. V.

Export- Label- Produce- Submit- Replace- Report Error- Update Holdings- Validate- Workflow-In Process

Example 8:4

```
tle:              Slavinë anëỹnskiiMł mir : problemy istorii i sovremennostKł
                       (paminë anëỹti Vladimira Konstantinovicha Volkova) /
                       [otvetstv. redaktor A.V. Karasev].
 blished/distributed:
                  Moskva : Institut slavinë anëỹnovedeniinë anëỹ RAN, 2006.
 ysical description:
                  134 p. : ill. ; 21 cm.
 ibject(s):       Volkov, V. K. (Vladimir Konstantinovich)
                  Slavic antiquities.
                  Civilization, Slavic.
 BN:              5757602015
                  9785757602011
 cord ID:         5490984

 cation:          YRL

 ll Number:       DJK27 .S54 2006
```

****
LA Library Catalog

APPENDIX

Example 8:5

Harvard University

HOLLIS CATALOG

- Search
- Expanded Search
- Command Search
- Results List
- Previous Searches
- Display Options

My Account/Re
Comments/Requ
Start (
?

Full Catalog Find Articles Journal Titles Digital Resources Reserves

ıll View of Record : FULL CATALOG

rint/Save/Send | Add to List | View List | Last Browse | Back to Results List

hoose format: Full view | Short view | MARC

ecord 1 out of 1

MT	BK
ƆR	nam 2200265Ia 4500
Ɔ1	010084663-7
Ɔ5	20070116205653.0
Ɔ8	061108s2006 ru o b 100 0 rusod
20	|a 5757602015
350	|a ocm75381849
40	|a OSU |c OSU
90	|a DJK27 |b .S54 2006
4500	|a Slavianskiĭ mir : |b problemy istorii i sovremennost' (pamiati Vladimira Konstantinovicha Volkova) / |c [otvetstv. redaktor A.V. Karasev].
60	|a Moskva : |b Institut slavianovedeniia RAN, |c 2006.
00	|a 134 p. : |b ill. ; |c 21 cm.
Ɔ0	|a At head of title: Pravitel'stvo Moskvy. Komitet mezhregional'nykh sviazeĭ i natsional'noĭ politiki g. Moskvy. Rossiĭskaia akademiia nauk. Institut slavianovedeniia. Slavianskiĭ fond Rossii.
;00	|a "Nauchnoe izdanie"--Colophon.
;04	|a Includes bibliographical references.
;50 0	|a Slavic antiquities.
;0010	|a Volkov, V. K. |q (Vladimir Konstantinovich)
;50 0	|a Civilization, Slavic.
'001	|a Karasev, A. V.
;YS	010084663

Example 8:6

```
_EADER  00000nam  2200289Ia 4500
001     75381849
003     OCoLC
005     20061211101503.0
008     061108s2006    ru o    b    100 0 rusod
020     5757602015
020     9785757602011
040     OSU|cOSU|dNOC
049     NOCC
090     DJK27|b.S5886 2006
245 00  Slav☐i☐anski☐ mir :|bproblemy istorii i sovremennost☐
        (pam☐i☐ati Vladimira Konstantinovicha Volkova) /
        |c[otvetstv. redaktor A.V. Karasev].
260     Moskva :|bInstitut slav☐i☐anovedeni☐i☐a RAN,|c2006.
300     134 p. :|bill. ;|c21 cm.
500     At head of title: Pravitel☐stvo Moskvy. Komitet
        mezhregional☐nykh sv☐i☐aze☐ i na☐t☐sional☐no☐ politiki g.
        Moskvy. Rossi☐ska☐i☐a akademi☐i☐a nauk. Institut
        slav☐i☐anovedeni☐i☐a. Slav☐i☐anski☐ fond Rossii.
500     "Nauchnoe izdanie"--Colophon.
504     Includes bibliographic references.
600 10  Volkov, V. K.|q(Vladimir Konstantinovich)
650  0  Slavic antiquities.
650  0  Civilization, Slavic.
700 1   Karasev, A. V.
994     CO|bNOC
```

Location	Call Number	Volume/Copy	Note	Status
Davis Library	DJK27 .S5886 2006			AVAILABLE

Catalog Home | Libraries & Collections | Hours | Interlibrary Loan | Other Catalogs | Libraries' Home
Please send comments and suggestions to the UNC Chapel Hill Web Catalog Tech Support Group.

Powered by Innovative Interfaces, Inc. 2003

APPENDIX

Example 8:7

Search Cornell

CATALOG
brary Gateway | Find it!:Articles Databases e-Journals Images |My Library |Ask a Librarian |Individual Libraries

NEW SEARCH | RETURN TO TITLES LIST | SEARCH HISTORY | PATRON INFO | REQUESTS | PREFERENCES | SAVED SEARCHES | BOOKBAG | INTERLIBRARY LOAN
BORROW DIRECT | HELP | REFWORKS | END SESSION

atabase Name: Cornell University Library
₃arch Request: Guided Keyword = (5757602015)[in]
₃arch Results: Displaying 1 of 1 entries

previous   next

Brief View   Long View   MARC View

Slavi͡a͡nskiĭ mir : problemy istorii i sovremennost' (pami͡a͡ti...

0 01186nam a2200277Ia 450
1 5954408
5 20061211190507.0
8 061108s2006 ru o b 100 0 rusod
5 __ |a (OCoLC)ocm75381849
0 __ |a OSU |c OSU
) __ |a *5757602015*
) __ |a DJK27 |b .S54 2006
) __ |a COOO
5 00 |a Slavi͡a͡nskiĭ mir : |b problemy istorii i sovremennost' (pami͡a͡ti Vladimira Konstantinovicha Volkova) / |c [otvetstv. redaktor A.V. Karasev].
) __ |a Moskva : |b Institut slavi͡a͡novedenii͡a͡ RAN, |c 2006.
) __ |a 134 p. : |b ill. ; |c 21 cm.
) __ |a At head of title: Pravitel'stvo Moskvy. Komitet mezhregional'nykh svi͡a͡zeĭ i nat͡s͡ional'noĭ politiki g. Moskvy. Rossiĭskai͡a͡ akademii͡a͡ nauk. Institut slavi͡a͡novedenii͡a͡. Slavi͡a͡nskiĭ fond Rossii.
) __ |a "Nauchnoe izdanie"--Colophon.
· __ |a Includes bibliographical references.
' 10 |a Volkov, V. K. |q (Vladimir Konstantinovich)
_0 |a Slavs |x Antiquities.

Example 8:8

50 _0 |a Civilization, Slavic.
00 1_ |a Karasev, A.V.
94 __ |a C0 |b COO
48 0_ |a 20061211 |b i |d nk31 |e lts |h appr
48 1_ |a 20061211 |b f |d nk31 |e lts |h appr

previous   next

Record Options		
Select Download Format Brief View	Format for Print/Save	Export to RefWorks
Save Search Query		
Enter your email address:		Email
Save results for later: Save To Bookbag		

New Search   Titles List Search History   Patron
Info   Requests   Preferences   SavedSearches   Bookbag   Interlibrary Loan   Borrow
Direct   Help   RefWorks   Exit

Ask a Librarian | Report a Problem Connecting | Send us Feedback
CU Info | Cornell University Homepage

APPENDIX

Example 8:9

```
_EADER 00000nam  2200349Ia 4500
 )01    75381849
 )03    OCoLC
 )05    20070102132149.0
 008    061108s2006    ru o      b    100 0 rusod
 020    5757602015
 035    .b62220457
 040    OSU|cOSU
 049    OSUU
 090    DJK27|b.S54 2006
 090    DJK27|b.S54 2006
 245 00 Slav□i□anski□ mir :|bproblemy istorii i sovremennost□
        (pam□i□ati Vladimira Konstantinovicha Volkova) /
        |c[otvetstv. redaktor A.V. Karasev]
 260    Moskva :|bInstitut slav□i□anovedeni□i□a RAN,|c2006
 300    134 p. :|bill. ;|c21 cm
 500    At head of title: Pravitel□stvo Moskvy. Komitet
        mezhregional□nykh sv□i□aze□ i na□t□sional□no□ politiki g.
        Moskvy. Rossi□ska□i□a akademi□i□a nauk. Institut
        slav□i□anovedeni□i□a. Slav□i□anski□ fond Rossii
 500    "Nauchnoe izdanie"--Colophon
 504    Includes bibliographical references
 600 10 Volkov, V. K.|q(Vladimir Konstantinovich)
 650  0 Slavic antiquities
 650  0 Civilization, Slavic
 700  1 Karasev, A. V
 910    xx2
 910    MARS
```

LOCATION	CALL NO.	YEAR	STATUS
ACK Stacks	DJK27 .S54 2006		AVAILABLE

© 2006, The Ohio State University Libraries.
1858 Neil Avenue Mall
Columbus, OH
43210-1286
Telephone: (614) 292-6154
Problems/Comments to Web Master
If you have difficulty accessing any portions of this site due to incompatibility with adaptive technology or need the information in an alternative form,
please contact Larry Allen.

Example 8:10

Detailed Record

☐ record 1 of 1 for search "5757602015"

| Item Information | Catalogue Record |

```
245: 00  : Slav T anskii mir :|bproblemy istorii i sovremennost' (pam'i`ati Vladimira
          Konstantinovicha Volkova) /|c[otvetstv. redaktor A.V. Karasev].
260:      : Moskva :|bInstitut slav`i`anovedeni`i`a RAN,|c2006.
300:      : 134 p. :|bill. ;|c21 cm.
600: 10   : Volkov, V. K.|q(Vladimir Konstantinovich)
650:  0   : Slavs|xAntiquities.
650:  0   : Civilization, Slavic.
500:      : At head of title: Pravitel'stvo Moskvy. Komitet
            mezhregional'nykh sv`i`azei i na`t`sional'noi politiki
            g. Moskvy. Rossiiska`i`a akademi`i`a nauk. Institut
            slav`i`anovedeni`i`a. Slav`i`anskii fond Rossii.
500:      : *Nauchnoe izdanie*--Colophon.
504:      : Includes bibliographical references.
020:      : 5757602015
020:      : 9785757602011
700:  1   : Karasev, A. V.
001:      : ocm75381849
```

6062212

APPENDIX 163

Example 9:1

Rec stat c	Entered 20020603		Replaced 20070220		
Type a	ELvl	Srce c	Audn	Ctrl	Lang rum
BLvl m	Form	Conf 0	Biog	MRec	Ctry rm
	Cont b	GPub	LitF 0	Indx 0	
Desc a	Ills a	Fest 0	DtSt m	Dates 2005 ,	9999

040		CSt ǂc STF
020		9738737257 (v. 1)
020		9789738737259 (v. 1)
041	0	rum ǂb eng ǂf eng
042		pcc
043		e-rm---
050	4	DR213 ǂb .H33 2005
090		ǂb
049		CGUA
245	0 0	Habitatul : ǂb răspunsuri la chestionarele Atlasului Etnografic Român / ǂc [coordonator genera Ion Ghinoiu].
260		București : ǂb Editura Enciclopedică, ǂc 2005-
300		v. : ǂb ill. ; ǂc 25 cm.
500		At head of title: Academia Română. Institutul de Etnografie și Folclor "C. Brăiloiu".
500		Vol. 4 contains introduction and table of contents in English.
546		Romanian; introduction and table of contents also in English.
505	1	vol. 1. Oltenia
650	0	Ethnology ǂz Romania.
650	0	Folklore ǂz Romania.
650	0	Holidays ǂz Romania.
651	0	Romania ǂx Social life and customs.
700	1	Ghinoiu, Ion.
710	2	Institutul de Etnografie și Folclor "C. Brăiloiu."
730	0	Atlasul Etnografic Român.

Delete   Export- Label- Produce- Submit- Replace- Report   Update   Validate-
Holdings-   Error-   Holdings-
                                                                        Workflow-In
                                                                        Process

Example 9:2

Rec stat c	Entered 20020603		Replaced 20070220		
Type a	ELvl	Srce c	Audn	Ctrl	Lang rum
BLvl m	Form	Conf 0	Biog	MRec	Ctry rm
	Cont b	GPub	LitF 0	Indx 0	
Desc a	Ills a	Fest 0	DtSt m	Dates 2005 ,	9999

```
040       CSt ǂc STF ǂd CGU
020       9738737257 (v. 1)
020       9789738737259 (v. 1)
041 0     rum ǂb eng ǂf eng
042       pcc
043       e-rm---
050     4 GT337 ǂb .H33 2005 ǂa DR213
049       CGUA
245 0 0   Habitatul : ǂb răspunsuri la chestionarele Atlasului Etnografic Român / ǂc [coordonator general
          Ion Ghinoiu].
260       Bucureşti : ǂb Editura Enciclopedică, ǂc 2005-
300       v. : ǂb ill. ; ǂc 25 cm.
500       At head of title: Academia Română. Institutul de Etnografie şi Folclor "C. Brăiloiu".
546       In Romanian; introduction and table of contents also in English.
505 1     vol. 1. Oltenia
650     0 Domestic space ǂz Romania.
650     0 Dwellings ǂz Romania.
650     0 Villages ǂz Romania.
650     0 Vernacular architecture ǂz Romania.
650     0 Architecture, Domestic ǂz Romania.
650     0 Farm buildings ǂz Romania.
650     0 Cemeteries ǂz Romania.
650     0 Romanians ǂx Dwellings.
650     0 Ethnology ǂz Romania.
651     0 Romania ǂx Social life and customs.
700 1     Ghinoiu, Ion.
710 2     Institutul de Etnografie şi Folclor "C. Brăiloiu".
730 0     Atlasul Etnografic Român.
```

Delete Holdings-	Export- C	Label-	Produce-	Submit- C	Replace-	Report Error-	Update Holdings-C	Validate-C
								Workflow-In Process

APPENDIX 165

Example 9:3

INTRODUCTION

This volume opens the series *THE HABITAT*[1] of the *CORPUS OF ROMANIAN ETHNOGRAPHICAL DOCUMENTS (DER)*.

The contained field information in this book was that written in the questionnaires Settlements – Household and Residence – Interior[2] applied for the ROMANIAN ETHNOGRAPHICAL ATLAS (1972-1982). The structure of the questionnaires (authors: Ion Ghinoiu, Monica Budiș, Cornelia Belcin Pleșca, Roswith Capesius, Paul Petrescu) aimed a detailed field research, to covering the main aspects of the themes, according to the existing stage of our discipline at that time. The coherence of the field - work was also eased by the drawing up and the logic of the setting of the chapters and questions; the open questions along with the ones suggesting alternative answers allowed to write down all data field. The sketches of the settlements, houses, households, outhouses, extensions, dependencies including interior and exterior technical and artistic details found in the questionnaires enriched this book, too.

The multitude and especially the thematic variety of the field data along with the development of the ethnological researches led to the necessity to setting a frame to organize the data, in order to allow a contextual reading. The purpose was to bring out the vertical of the semantic levels, with it different degrees of generalization, along with the possible correspondences between various themes and sub-themes in the same horizontal level, no matter the nature of the data. It was necessary to establishing the order of the presentation of the main chapters, the very same ones of the questionnaires. Therefore, it was decided to begin with the complete territory of the village, the estate, continued by the precincts, then the household, area of the family habitation. The residence was the next, till the details of the interior and then, the correspondent of the precincts of the living, the precincts of the dead, the cemetery. The information considered to having a more complex level of characterization of the settlements were included in the first chapter, that of general elements. Many of the primary data have a multi-disciplinary character, such as those regarding the elements of the constructions, where architectural details can be find along with local geographical characteristics as the relief, materials, art elements: form, chromatics, adornment.

The first design of the volume was structured in large chapters and sub-chapters, beginning with the large unit till the detail. As the questionnaires were scoured along, data appeared

---

[1] *DER* conține următoarele serii: *Habitatul, Ocupațiile, Tehnica populară, Arta populară, Obiceiuri și Mitologie*. Ordinea apariției volumelor din fiecare serie: vol. I *Oltenia*; vol. II *Banat. Crișana. Maramureș*; vol. III *Transilvania*; vol IV *Moldova*; vol. V *Muntenia. Dobrogea*.

[2] Chestionarul de Așezări – Gospodărie, autori: Ion Ghinoiu, Monica Budiș; chestionarul de Locuință – Interior, autori: Paul Petrescu, Roswith Capesius, Cornelia Pleșca.

Example 9:4

TABLE OF CONTENTS

```
FOREWARD ............................................................................. XIII
INTRODUCTION ..................................................................... XVII
Tehnical Note ........................................................................ XXIX

Part I – THE SETTLEMENT ....................................................... 1

GENERAL ISSUES ..................................................................... 1
    Social-Historical Category ..................................................... 1
    Founding Legends ............................................................... 2
    Local History Data ............................................................... 5

THE VILLAGE ESTATE ............................................................... 7
    Customs to establish the Estate of the Village ........................ 7
    The Boundaries between the Villages .................................... 8
    The Individual Boundaries .................................................... 9
    General Toponyms ............................................................. 11
    Particular Toponyms .......................................................... 17
    The Techniques of the Measurement of the Land ................. 28
        Systems of Dividing the Land ......................................... 28
    The Form of the Property of the Land .................................. 33
    The Way to farm the Land .................................................. 33
    Main Occupations .............................................................. 36
    Secondary Occupations ..................................................... 37
    Handcraftsmen .................................................................. 38
    Markets ............................................................................. 39
    Trading of the Products ..................................................... 42
    Shifting for the Work ......................................................... 44
    Properties on the Territories of other Villages ..................... 47
    Signs of Habitation in the Estate of the Village ................... 48
    Buildings and Implements ................................................. 49
```

Example 9:5

X   Habitatul

THE PRECINCTS OF THE VILLAGE	54
Customs to establish the Precincts of the Village	54
The Area	54
The Place of the Precincts	54
The Form	55
The Morphological Structure	57
Toponyms	57
Changes of the Precincts of the Village	59
Melioration	61
Drinking Water Supplies	62
Finding out the Water Supplies	64
The Way to use	64
Customs	65
The Inhabitants	66
Number of the Inhabitants	66
Number of the Households	66
Number of the Families	66
The Origin of the Inhabitants	67
Kin	67
The Parts of the Village	70
The Nicknames of the Inhabitants	73
Duties of the Village	73
Part II – THE HOUSEHOLD	75
The Yard	75
Habitation Units within the same Household	77
The Enclosures	79
The Gates	85
The Gardens	87
The Outbuildings	89
Shelters for the Grains	89
Shelters for the Animals	96
Ways to shelter the Forage and the Straws	100
Shelters for Carts and Tools	102
Other Buildings	104
Building Materials and Techniques	108
General Issues	108
The Foundation and the Sole (Romanian *talpă*)	108
The Walls	109
The Ceiling	113

Example 9:6

Contents	XI
The Roof and the Framework	113
The Cover	117
By Categories of Shelters	122
Shelters for the Grains	122
Shelters for the Animals	124
Shelters for the Forage and Straws	128
Shelters for Carts and Tools	128

Part III – THE HOUSE 129

The Orientation	129
Designs	131
Changing the Initial Design of the House	150
Proportions	152
The Porch	154
The Balcony	158
Building Materials and Techniques	161
The Foundation and the Sole (Romanian *talpă*)	161
The Floor	166
The Walls	167
The Ceiling	176
The Roof, the Framework	178
The Cover	183
Artistic Values of the House	188

THE INTERIOR 197

Ways to arrange the Rooms	197
The Hearth	203
The Stove	206
The Oven	210
The Installations to evacuate the Smoke	215
Objects and Tools connected to the Hearth, Oven, Stove	218
Ways to lighting	223
Pieces for Housekeeping	224
Pieces for Storage	225
Resting Spaces and Pieces	228
Representation Spaces and Pieces	233

THE SEMIBURIED HOUSE, THE COTTAGE 243

THE HOUSE BUILT ON LEVEL DIFFERENCES AND/OR HIGH SOCLE 246

APPENDIX

Example 9:7

XII *Habitatul*
TWO LEVELS HOUSE 249

Part IV – THE CEMETERY 255

    The Place where the Dead were buried 255
    The Dividing of the Cemetery 256
    The Inheritance of the Burial Place 256
    The Place of the Burial of the Strangers 257
    The Place of the Burial of the Malefactors Self - murderers, the ones
        belonging to other Cults 257
    Crosses for the Dead 257

GLOSSARY 259

Appendix 1: List of Researched Villages in Oltenia 273
Appendix 2: Villages, Researchers and Informers 275

Example 10:1

Rec stat n	Entered 20040623		Replaced 20061005		
Type a	ELvl	Srce c	Audn	Ctrl	Lang pol
BLvl m	Form	Conf 0	Biog	MRec	Ctry pl
	Cont	GPub	LitF 0	Indx 1	
Desc a	Ills a	Fest 0	DtSt s	Dates 2004 ,	

```
010       2005443531
040       CSt ǂc STF ǂd DLC
020       8389115158
020       9788389115157
041 0     pol ǂa eng
042       pcc
043       e-pl---
050 0 0   DK4122 ǂb .P658 2004
090       ǂb
049       CGUA
245 0 0   Polskie instytucje za granicą : ǂb przewodnik po zbiorach archiwalnych / ǂc opracowała Anna
          Krochmal.
260       Warszawa : ǂb Naczelna Dyrekcja Archiwów Państwowych, ǂc 2004.
300       302 p. : ǂb col. ill. ; ǂc 24 cm.
500       At head of title: Rada Dziedzictwa Archiwalnego. Naczelna Dyrekcja Archiwów Państwowych.
546       Pref. also in English.
500       Includes indexes.
650    0  Poles ǂz Foreign countries ǂx Intellectual life.
650    0  Poles ǂz Foreign countries ǂx Societies, etc.
650    0  Poles ǂx Education (Higher) ǂz Foreign countries.
650    0  Schools, Polish ǂz Foreign countries.
650    0  Learned institutions and societies ǂz Poland ǂx History ǂy 20th century.
650    0  Poles ǂz Foreign countries ǂv Archives.
700 1     Krochmal, Anna.
710 1     Poland. ǂb Rada Dziedzictwa Archiwalnego.
710 1     Poland. ǂb Naczelna Dyrekcja Archiwów Państwowych.
```

Delete Holdings-	Export- Label- Produce- Submit- Replace- Report Error-	Update Holdings-	Validate- Workflow-In Process

Example 10:2

Rec stat c	Entered 20040623		Replaced 20070227		
Type a	ELvl	Srce c	Audn	Ctrl	Lang pol
BLvl m	Form	Conf 0	Biog	MRec	Ctry pl
	Cont	GPub	LitF 0	Indx 1	
Desc a	Ills a	Fest 0	DtSt s	Dates 2004 ,	

010	2005443531
040	CSt ǂc STF ǂd DLC ǂd CGU
020	8389115158
020	9788389115157
041 0	pol ǂa eng
042	pcc
043	e-pl---
050 0 0	DK4122 ǂb .P658 2004
049	CGUA
245 0 0	Polskie instytucje za granicą : ǂb przewodnik po zbiorach archiwalnych / ǂc opracowała Anna Krochmal.
260	Warszawa : ǂb Naczelna Dyrekcja Archiwów Państwowych, ǂc 2004.
300	302 p. : ǂb col. ill. ; ǂc 24 cm.
500	At head of title: Rada Dziedzictwa Archiwalnego. Naczelna Dyrekcja Archiwów Państwowych.
546	Pref. also in English.
500	Includes indexes.
650 0	Poles ǂz Foreign countries ǂx Archives ǂv Guidebooks.
650 0	Poles ǂz Foreign countries ǂx Societies, etc. ǂx Archives ǂv Guidebooks.
650 0	Schools, Polish ǂz Foreign countries ǂx Archives ǂv Guidebooks.
700 1	Krochmal, Anna.
710 1	Poland. ǂb Rada Dziedzictwa Archiwalnego.
710 1	Poland. ǂb Naczelna Dyrekcja Archiwów Państwowych.

Delete Holdings-	Export- C	Label-	Produce-	Submit- C	Replace-	Report Error-	Update Holdings-	Validate-C Workflow-In Process

Example 10:3

Rec stat c	Entered 20040714		Replaced 20060529			
Type a	ELvl M	Srce d	Audn	Ctrl		Lang pol
BLvl m	Form	Conf 0	Biog	MRec		Ctry pl
	Cont	GPub	LitF 0	Indx 0		
Desc i	Ills	Fest 0	DtSt s	Dates 2004 ,		

```
040      NUKAT ǂb pol ǂc NUKAT
020      8389115158
020      9788389115157
029 0    NUKAT ǂb zz2004950044
090      ǂb
049      CGUA
100 1    Krochmal, Anna ǂd (1965- ).
245 0 0  Polskie instytucje za granicą : ǂb przewodnik po zbiorach archiwalnych / ǂc oprac. Anna
         Krochmal ; Rada Dziedzictwa Archiwalnego, Naczelna Dyrekcja Archiwów Państwowych.
260      Warszawa : ǂb NDAP - Wydział Wydawnictw, ǂc 2004.
300      302, [2] s., [15] s. tabl. : ǂb il. (gł. kolor.) ; ǂc 24 cm.
504      Indeksy.
546      Wstęp także ang.
650   7  Polacy ǂx zbiory archiwalne ǂz za granicą ǂv wydawnictwa informacyjne. ǂ2 jhpk
650   7  Polacy ǂx życie intelektualne ǂx zbiory archiwalne ǂz za granicą ǂv wydawnictwa
         informacyjne. ǂ2 jhpk
651   7  Polska ǂx emigracja i imigracja ǂx zbiory archiwalne ǂv wydawnictwa informacyjne. ǂ2 jhpk
```

Delete holdings-	Export- Label- Produce- Submit- Replace- Report Error-	Update Holdings-	Validate- Workflow-In Process

About the Author

David Bade is a Senior Librarian at the University of Chicago's Joseph Regenstein Library where he is responsible for the cataloguing of Eastern European publications. He studied linguistics (minor in Arabic) and librarianship at the University of Illinois. His present research is focused on the processes of misunderstanding, mystifying and mythologizing technologies and how this allows a technocratic elite to turn convivial tools into tools for control and exploitation. The communicative and linguistic aspects of this process—from managerial rhetoric to spamming—are the subjects of work in press and in progress.

www.ingramcontent.com/pod-product-compliance
Lightning Source LLC
Chambersburg PA
CBHW052051220426
43663CB00012B/2526